John Wesley Butler

Sketches of Mexico in Prehistoric, Primitive, Colonial, and Modern Times

John Wesley Butler

Sketches of Mexico in Prehistoric, Primitive, Colonial, and Modern Times

ISBN/EAN: 9783337155414

Printed in Europe, USA, Canada, Australia, Japan

Cover: Foto ©Thomas Meinert / pixelio.de

More available books at **www.hansebooks.com**

Sketches of Mexico

IN

PREHISTORIC, PRIMITIVE, COLONIAL,
AND MODERN TIMES.

Lectures

AT

Syracuse University

ON THE

Graves Foundation

1894

By REV. JOHN W. BUTLER, D.D.

Twenty years resident in Mexico

NEW YORK: HUNT & EATON
CINCINNATI: CRANSTON & CURTS
1894

TO

MY VENERABLE FATHER,

THE REV. WILLIAM BUTLER, D.D.,

WHOSE VOICE AND PEN, FOR MORE THAN HALF A CENTURY,

IN IRELAND AND IN INDIA,

IN THE UNITED STATES AND IN MEXICO,

HAVE PLEADED ELOQUENTLY FOR THE WORLD'S REDEMPTION,
THESE MEXICAN SKETCHES ARE

AFFECTIONATELY DEDICATED BY

HIS SON.

SYLLABUS.

LECTURE I.
SOURCES OF INFORMATION.
Spanish cruelty. The heroic Cuautemoc. Hieroglyphics and picture paintings. Sacrilegious vandalism.................page 1

LECTURE II.
ORIGIN OF THE MEXICANS.
With a review of the autochthonic and migratory theories concerning the first inhabitants of the western continent. Noah's grandson. Did Solomon draw material for the building of the temple from Mexico?... 33

LECTURE III.
PREHISTORIC MEXICANS.
Mexico the cradle of American civilization. St. Thomas and the cross in Mexico..................................... 81

LECTURE IV.
EARLY MEXICANS AND THEIR HISTORY.
The Toltecs. Nahuas, Chichimecs, Aztecs, etc. Their migrations. Their civilizations. The Fair God. " The Chair of God," or the Ark of the Covenant. The Mexican ensign and Bishop Simpson... 121

LECTURE V.
THE MOCTEZUMAS AND THE KING DAVID OF MEXICO.
Tenochtitlan. Origin of the word Mexico. Huitzilopochtli. The Athens of Anahuac. The King David of Mexico. Mocte-

zuma I. "Fight till death." Spread of his empire. Moctezuma II. Mexico's great population. Court life and palaces of pleasure. Teocalli. Human sacrifices. The exaggerations of Prescott and others. Moctezuma and evil auguries. The European on the coast. Spaniards and greed of gold. Europe in the sixteenth century. Original copy of the Bull of Alexander VI... 163

LECTURE VI.
THE ARRIVAL OF THE SPANIARDS.

Hernan Cortez and Luther, "the infernal beast." The cruel conqueror. Unique missionary methods. "Apostolic blows and knocks." "Without a parallel in history." The Tlaxcalan republic. Why Cortez succeeded against such odds. Fall of Moctezuma. Indian eloquence. "Tax collectors, priests, and miners"... 199

LECTURE VII.
INDEPENDENCE AND THE CONSTITUTION OF 1857.

Colonial times. The King of Spain and the holy father. Priest and soldier despoiling homes. The oppressive legislation of Spain. The Inquisition. Hidalgo and his cry of independence. Death of the hero and triumph of his cause. Santa Ana. Constitution of 1857. Separation of Church and State.... 239

LECTURE VIII.
NEW LIFE IN MEXICO.

The Mexican War. General Grant's condemnation of the same. Extension of slavery. Ten millions for Texas. Reform and Benito Juarez. Expulsion of the Jesuits, nuns, and sisters of charity. A contrast—the promoters of the French intervention and the present condition of Mexico. Protestant missions. Latest statistics. Incidents. Methodism and her mission in our sister republic................................... 277

INTRODUCTION.

BY LEROY M. VERNON, D.D.,
Dean of the College of Fine Arts.

THESE lecture sketches are an opportune and important contribution to the literature regarding our next-door neighbor on the south. Our national neighbors, like citizen ones, are interesting to us in many ways, and by us should be respectfully studied and thoroughly known. Yet Mexico, much as it and the United States have acted and reacted upon each other, is but very imperfectly understood by the great majority of our people. This is due partly to its language, so different from our own, partly to Mexico's relative minority, exaggerated, perhaps, by our prejudices, and partly still to the comparatively limited commercial exchanges hitherto between the two peoples. But most of these conditions, however formed or deformed, are now being sensibly modified in themselves or in their effects, and the two neighbor nations are gradually coming into closer relations, politically, commercially, and otherwise. Americans, therefore, have increasing need and occasion to familiarize themselves with the history, the institutions, the language, and the character of the Mexican people, with their progress, their genius, and their aspirations, with their possibilities and prospects.

Of books on Mexico published in English during the present generation the most were written by hasty travelers or conventional compilers, whose views and portraitures are inevitably immature, partial, or exaggerated. Their more important and characteristic qualities, gifts, and aims, lie too deeply in the nature of the Mexican people to be clearly discerned and duly appreciated by the passing tourist or the nonresident compiler. The richest treasures of information, too, regarding their traditions and history, their struggles, conflicts, and achievements, are tomes in Spanish, Italian, or other languages not often either accessible or intelligible to such writers.

Our present author, however, fortunately free from such obstructive and misleading conditions and disabilities, came to his work with peculiar advantages, personal fitness, and zest. Dr. Butler has an easy mastery of the Spanish language and a close familiarity with the daily life, the habits, and the customs of the people. He has lived and labored among them in the city of Mexico for twenty years, always a close observer and a careful student of their character and life and of all that relates to them. He has mingled with the people of all ranks and classes, from the president and his counselors to the provincial Indian in his rude hut. He has seen the Mexicans in their workday clothes and in

INTRODUCTION. ix

their galaday garb, in their toils, their sorrows, and their joys, at their worship, in their festivities, and in their diversions. He has traveled extensively about the country and is familiar with its topography, its antiquities, its vast resources, and its advancing improvements. Thus he had ample qualifications before he took occasion to lecture on Mexico.

There is much interesting material here relating to the first inhabitants and to the earlier institutions, to memorable incidents and to controlling events in Mexican history, rarely presented, if ever before, to American readers. Graphic indeed are the pictures Dr. Butler gives us of the Moctezumas, of Cortez and his followers, and of the Quixotic enterprise of Maximilian and Napoleon III. His representation of the actual republic of Mexico, of its founders and chief factors, of its policy, its liberal and patriotic spirit, and its great achievements already, as of its bright prospects, is most opportune and valuable. The style of these sketches is easy, lucid, and straightforward. Those who followed the lectures closely in their delivery at the University this spring were increasingly interested from the beginning to the end, pleased equally with their current popular style and with their richness and variety of matter.

Incidentally Dr. Butler treats of the remains of ancient cities and of the monumental memorials of former civilizations, many of them until recently unknown, and in regard to which, with the times and people they represent, there are no historic records nor any credible traditions. The account of these venerable ruins, of strange idols, of the pictorial language on some stone memorials and of other antiquities, will be to many a most suggestive and engaging feature of this interesting volume. This matter is the more attractive now because, since the delivery of the lectures, a company of American explorers have sent us telegraphic news of their discovery of the vast ruins and remains of two great cities among the Sierra Madre Mountains. Unquestionably a rich field awaits the archæologist in many yet unexplored parts of Mexico. It was Dr. Butler's rare fortune, in his necessary travel, quite incidentally to discover and to bring to the notice of the governmental authorities an ancient idol of colossal proportions lying in the bed of a mountain stream. Although the Indians of the locality had seen it, it was wholly unknown to the officers of the country, to the learned and to the Mexican antiquarians.

A country of such extent and resources, of a history so eventful, of so abundant prehistoric memorials and monuments, of so progressive a government and people, of such present energy and thrift, and of such prospective growth and power well deserves to be more fully and more widely known—deserves also a full share of our individual as of our national consideration and comity.

Syracuse, N. Y., May 25, 1894.

LECTURE I.

SOURCES OF INFORMATION.

SKETCHES OF MEXICO.

LECTURE I.

SOURCES OF INFORMATION.

ABOUT midway between the National Palace and the historic Castle of Chapultepec (the "West Point" of Mexico) on the beautiful Paseo, or drive, laid out by the unfortunate Carlotta, Archduchess of Austria, stands an imposing monument which excites the admiration of the multitudes and awakens the spirit of inquiry in many a thoughtful mind. We do not refer to the great equestrian statue of Charles IV, cast by Tolsa in 1803, which Baron Humboldt declares to be the finest of its kind in all the world, next to the famous Marcus Aurelius in the city of Rome, as it is the most elegant and possibly the largest bronze statue ever made in America; nor do we refer to the Columbus monument donated to the city in 1877 by Señor Antonio Escandon, with its solid base of basalt, octagonal in form, its square pedestal of Russian jasper bearing four basso-relievos, and four life-size figures of as many Spanish friars who came with the conquerors, and on the top a graceful statue of Christopher Columbus, with the left hand drawing the veil from the western world and the right raised as if invoking the benediction of Heaven upon his hazardous enterprise; but we refer to the most significant and finest of them all, the one which stands in the second *glorieta* (circle) of the Paseo. Here the Mexican architect Jimenez has erected a magnificent memorial. It stands on a slight elevation above the drive with four short stairways leading up, the entrance to which, in each case, is guarded by a bronze leopard. Just above the basaltic pedestal on two sides are found inscriptions, and on the other two reliefs. As you approach from the east the inscription which first meets the sight, translated, reads as follows:

"To the memory of Cuautemoc and the warriors who fought heroically in defense of their country, in 1521."

The inscription on the west side tells us that the monument was ordered by General Porfirio Diaz, in 1876, and finished during the presidency of General Manuel Gonzalez, in 1883. On the north side you may see the well-executed relief which represents Captain Diego de Olguin delivering his royal prisoner to the Spanish conqueror. On the south side

SOURCES OF INFORMATION. 5

is r presented a scene which might well cause every son of Spain to blush with shame.

Cuautemoc and his cousin, Tlacopan, Prince of Tezcoco, having both fallen into the hands of their heartless conquerors, have been bound hand and foot, laid upon stone slabs while their fettered feet hang over flames of fire. In this way the voracious Cortez hoped to compel his victims to reveal the place of their hidden treasures. More than three hundred years have passed since this most atrocious deed took place, and the world to-day, more than ever, realizes the real motive animating the hearts of Cortez and his followers, notwithstanding their constant profession of a desire to propagate "the Christian faith." Surely "the love of gold" was the root of this evil.

This bas-relief brings to mind another historic fact, in itself as noble and inspiring as the former was disgraceful and infamous. As the excruciating pains ran from the soles of his feet to the crown of his head the Aztec monarch suffered all without a word or even a sigh of complaint. But the Prince of Tezcoco called out to him in his extreme agony, "Sire, seest thou not how I suffer?" The indomitable monarch answered, "Am I in a bath or in delight?" or, as it has been more poetically rendered, "Thinkest thou I am on a bed of roses?" No wonder the cousin took new courage and that some of the Spaniards began to vacillate concerning their cruel treatment.

The suffering emperor seemed to understand all and cried out to them, "Do not be weary; he who has resisted famine, death, and the wrath of the gods is not capable of humiliating himself now like a weak woman; the treasury of the kings of Mexico I submerged in the lake four days before the siege of the city, and you will never find it."

The second part of the pedestal contains the names of four heroes and representations of Aztec shields and arms. On the third section, which is beautifully ornamented with ancient symbols, stands a large bronze statue of the heroic Cuautemoc, who, at the early age of twenty-four years, was made king of a kingdom which flourished ages before Charles IV ever ruled or Columbus ever dreamed of seeking new worlds.

The origin and history of the people who could produce such noble specimens of manhood, as well as the history of their contemporaneous and succeeding nations, claim our attention at this time. We propose also to speak of their manners and customs, languages and religions, and, after devoting considerable space to these primitive tribes, we will pass under review the ever-enchanting Homeric

SOURCES OF INFORMATION. 7

story of the Conquest, the not less interesting colonial times, the heroic and successful struggle for independence and autonomy, and the more protracted struggle for freedom from priestcraft and papal rule, in which Louis Napoleon, Pius IX, and Maximilian, Archduke of Austria, each played such important parts.

We will then look into modern Mexico, with its new life and ever-growing development, the origin and marvelous spread of Protestant missions, their utility, and the present outlook and future prospects of this most interesting and wonderful country.

That this continent was inhabited centuries before the so-called discovery of America by Columbus in 1492, or by the Northmen from Scandinavia—which latter discovery, according to Humboldt, took place about the year 1000—is no longer a disputed question. Empires with thousands, and in some cases millions, of subjects rose in splendor on American soil, flourished for centuries, and passed away, only to be succeeded by others more numerous or powerful than they. Mexico was the home of some of the most interesting and lasting of those empires.

It is greatly to be regretted that the sacrilegious vandalism and mistaken religious zeal of the Spanish conquerors has robbed the student of history of records which to-day ought to be found in the universities and museums of our sister republic. Their existence would have opened up a rich field of study, as fascinating as any which the masters of Roman and Greek literature have placed in the libraries and curriculums of American colleges. The Aztecs and contemporaneous as well as antecedent tribes commemorated passing events by elaborate sculpture and picture painting.

Brantz Mayer, for some time secretary of the American Legation in Mexico, in his valuable work justly remarks: "One of the most disgraceful destructions of property recorded in history is that which was accomplished in Mexico by the first archbishop of New Spain, Juan de Zumarraga. He collected from all quarters, but especially from Tezcoco, where the national archives were deposited, all the Indian manuscripts he could discover, and, causing them to be piled in a great heap in the market place of Tlatelolco, he burned all these precious records, which under the skillful interpretations of competent natives, might have relieved the early history of the Aztecs from the obscurity with which it is now clouded. The superstitious soldiery eagerly imitated the pious example of this prelate, and emulated each other in destroying all the books, charts, and papers which bore hieroglyphic signs, whose import, they had been taught to believe, was

SOURCES OF INFORMATION. 9

as sacrilegiously symbolic and pernicious as that of the idols they had already hurled from the Indian temples."*

This wholesale destruction was doubtless due to the fact that the priests mistook these pictured figures to be representatives of heathen deities. Father Bartholomew de las Casas admits, in his *Historia Apologetica*, that they were actuated by the fear that in matters of religion the existence of these books would be injurious.

Be this as it may, "The infamous crime committed against the cause of knowledge and the irreparable injury done to the natives, their successors, and to the students of history for all time, by the destruction of those valuable manuscripts, must ever remain an unerasable blot upon the name of the early Church in Mexico, and must be ranked with the worst deeds of Goths and Vandals. Juan de Zumarraga, the chief of these sacrilegious destroyers, who committed the annals of the Mexican States publicly to the flames in his tour of the principal cities of the country, will ever be remembered with proper contempt." †

These sad facts are sustained by Torquemada, by Ixtlilxochitl, as quoted by Lord Kingsborough in

* Hartford edition, 1851, p. 92.
† J. T. Short's *The North Americans of Antiquity*, p. 429.

his monumental work on *Mexican Antiquities*, by Prescott, Sahagun, Clavigero, Humboldt, and by many others.

The value of these hieroglyphics and picture paintings will appear to us when we remember that the aboriginals of Mexico recorded by these means everything which they deemed worthy of preservation, and the art was greatly prized and zealously cultivated by them, but was thus lost to humanity forever.

Bancroft, from whose extensive works we shall frequently quote in these Lectures, says:

"The written records included national, historic, and traditional annals, names and genealogical tables of kings and nobles, lists and tribute rolls of provinces and cities, land titles, law codes, court records, the calendar and succession of feasts, religious ceremonies of the temple service, names and attributes of the gods, the mysteries of augury and soothsaying, with some description of social customs, mechanical employments, and educational processes. The preparation and guardianship of records of the higher class, such as historical annals and ecclesiastical mysteries, were under the control of the highest ranks of the priesthood, and such records, comparatively few in number, were carefully guarded in the temple archives of a few of the larger cities.

SOURCES OF INFORMATION.

These writings were a sealed book to the masses, and even to the educated classes, who looked with superstitious reverence on the priestly writers and their magic scrolls. It is probable that the art as applied to names of persons and places or to ordinary records was understood by all educated persons, although by no means a popular art, and looked upon as a great mystery by the common people. The hieroglyphics were painted in bright colors on long strips of cotton cloth, prepared skins, or maguey paper, generally the latter rolled up or, preferably, folded fanlike into convenient books called "amatl," and furnished often with thin wooden covers. The same characters were also carved on the stones of public buildings, and probably also in some cases on natural cliffs. The early authorities are unanimous in crediting these people with the possession of a hieroglyphic system sufficiently perfect to meet all their requirements."

Fortunately, however, the learned Dr. Robertson, of the University of Edinburgh, who lived and wrote in the eighteenth century, is not quite correct when he says, " In consequence of this fanatical zeal of the monks we have totally lost every intelligence of the most remote events contained in these rude monuments, and there does not remain a single trace of the policy and ancient revolutions of the empire excepting those which are derived from tradition or from some fragments of their historical pictures which escaped the barbarous search of Zumarraga. It appears evident from the experience of all nations that the memory of past events cannot be long preserved, nor transmitted with fidelity, by tradition. The Mexican pictures, which are supposed to have served as annals of their empire, are few in number and of ambiguous meaning. Thus, from the uncertainty of the one and the obscurity of the others, we are obliged to avail ourselves of such intelligence as can be gleaned from the imperfect materials which are found scattered in the Spanish writers."

We find a list of some three hundred different works (largely Spanish and Portuguese) published in the first part of Dr. Robertson's valuable History, which were consulted by him, and hence we cannot understand how he was so seriously deceived. He seems, like many others who never visited the country, to have overlooked entirely the histories written by the Indians themselves, and to have failed in appreciation of the historical pictures, which in some cases were hidden away by the natives, and in other cases were reproduced by their artists at the time.

Clavigero, a recognized authority, declares that

SOURCES OF INFORMATION. 13

"at the time the missionaries performed that unfortunate burning of the pictures many Acolhuan, Mexican, Tepanecan, Tlascalan, and other historians were living, and employed themselves to repair the loss of these monuments. This they in part accomplished by painting new pictures or making use of our characters, which they had learned, and instructing by word of mouth their preachers in their antiquity, that it might be preserved in their writings, which Motolinia, Olmos, and Sahagun have done." *

From the same author we learn of the existence of five valuable collections of these paintings:

1. The Mendoza collection. This collection was composed of sixty-three Mexican paintings secured by one of the early bishops of Mexico, Antonio Mendoza, for Charles V. The vessel in which they were shipped was captured on the high seas by French pirates and carried to France. Here they fell into the hands of Thevenot, a noted geographer, whose heirs sold them at a great price to the chaplain of the British embassy, who sent them to his native land and possibly to the British Museum. The first twelve contain the history of the foundation of Mexico, the years and conquest of the kings; the

* *History of Mexico*, Abbé F. S. Clavigero, Richmond edition, 1833, p. 33.

thirty-four following represent the tributary cities and the quantity and species of their tributes; and the remaining seventeen explained a part of the education of their youth and their civil government.

2. The Vatican collection. Acosta mentions such a collection, which is doubtless still in existence.

3. The Vienna collection. This consists of eight paintings, which were presented by the King of Portugal to Clement VII. From the pope they passed into the hands of others, and finally were presented to Leopold, the emperor.

4. The Siguenza collection. This learned antiquarian of Mexico is said to have made a large collection of valuable paintings, part of which he inherited from the famous Ixtlilxochitl, who in turn inherited them from his ancestors, the kings of Tezcoco. Siguenza, on his death, left all to the Jesuit College of St. Peter and St. Paul in the city of Mexico. They, in common with all Church property, were confiscated by the republican government in 1859.

5. The Boturini collection—called his historical Indian Museum—was composed of many maps, hieroglyphics on skin and maguey paper. These were confiscated by the colonial government and deposited in the Royal University, founded in 1553. It is said this seemingly arbitrary act was due to

the fact that many of these precious treasures were being lost through the carelessness of the Boturini family.

The remains of this and the Siguenza collection are now in the possession of the government in the city of Mexico, and, doubtless, make the most valuable of existing collections.

Specimens of the picture writings are also found in some of the old Indian families of Mexico.* Others have found their way into libraries of Europe as well as in the United States. At least one original and several duplicates may be seen in the Smithsonian Institution.

Mr. F. A. Ober says that during one of his three visits to Mexico he heard of one " over sixty feet long, a narrow strip, folded after the manner of a book, with wooden strips at the extremities, which formed the covers when closed."

On this subject in general the same author adds:

"Although the best and most valuable Aztec manuscripts or picture paintings were destroyed by Zumarraga, first bishop of Mexico, some remained, and others, as soon as the Spaniards became sensible of this error, were produced by learned Indians

---

* Señor Icazbalceta, Señor Alfredo Chavero, Señor Abadeario, and other Mexican antiquarians own some of these now priceless relics.

by order of the viceroy. We know that the Mexicans were very apt at depicting scenes and representing occurrences, and that the landing of the Spaniards in 1519, with all its attendant circumstances, was transmitted to Moctezuma by his skillful painters before the bustle of that event had subsided." *

In the great book by Lord Kingsborough we may find the various "codices" produced in facsimile, with all the bright, fadeless colors of the originals. "I have in my possession a lithographed chart in black and white, of some five meters in length, prepared by direction of that indefatigable archæologist, Mr. Squires, so well known as an authority on Central America. Four 'maps,' or charts, are given; the first, a history of the sovereign States and the kings of Acolhuacan, is a nonchronological map, belonging to the collection of Boturini. It is on prepared skin, and represents the genealogy of the Chichimeque emperors from Tlotzin to the last king, Don Fernando Ixtlilxochitl, and has a number of paragraphs in Nahuatl, or Mexican. It belonged, according to an inscription on the back, to Don Diego Pimental, descendant of King Mezalhualcoyotl. It gives a summary of the wars, pestilences, etc., which destroyed the Toltecs, and depicts the

* *Travels in Mexico*, p. 316.

journeyings of the barbarous Chichimecs who invaded the valley of Anahuac, and finally established themselves at Tezcoco. I produce here fragments of two of the pictures showing them as living in the caves of Chicomoztoc, their subsequent migration, and their barbarous nomadic life, when they subsisted entirely upon the chase and the wild plants of the field. The second series pictures them as having settled at Tezcoco and engaged in the pursuits of agriculture, being surrounded by figures of the maguey, cultivated cactus, and other plants. The third gives us a glimpse of their later life, after they had assimilated the remnant of the Toltecs remaining in the valley and had learned from them the arts for which the latter people had been distinguished, such as the casting of metals, the manufacture of jewelry, copper utensils, etc. The most valuable of the series is called 'Map Tepechpan,' also one of the Boturini collection, and consists of synchronous annals of the principalities of Tepechpan and Mexico, commencing with the year 1298 and ending at the conquest, subsequently extended by less skillful hands to 1596.

"Like the two manuscripts before spoken of, these go back to the savage era of the Chichimecs, but give the leading events in the Tepechpan and Mexican tribes until the establishment of the Mexican empire, thence relating exclusively to the latter. Wars, earthquakes, volcanic eruptions, inundations, etc., are all accurately recorded under the date of their occurrence. The coming of Cortez, the death of Montezuma, the murder of his nephew, and the accession of Guatemotzin are all intelligibly set down here in unmistakable characters."

We are aware that tradition is not always a safe guide to follow, it is so likely to be distorted; but we also think that many learned writers in our own country as well as Europe make a great mistake in almost completely ignoring traditional help in the study of the American question. This is especially so with those who study the question "from afar," and publish their opinions without ever visiting the cradles of these traditions and seeing for themselves such monumental evidences as are often found in support of what is generally called tradition. For example, the learned Dr. D. G. Brinton, of the University of Pennsylvania, has recently published a volume of most valuable essays.* One of these he entitles "The Toltecs and Their Fabulous Empire." We cannot resist the conviction that the doctor would greatly modify his opinions if he would only

---

* *Essays of an Americanist*, Daniel G. Brinton, A.M., M.D. Philadelphia, 1890. The same author published in 1868 *The Myths of the New World*.

spend a few months in Mexico and stand in the presence of mute yet powerful and mysterious relics which are seen on every hand.

For instance, he calls the Toltecs, as currently related to ancient Mexican history, "a myth" (p. 83), and the Toltec empire "a baseless fable" (p. 85), and exclaims concerning the famous ruins of Tula, "I fear that they are to be sought nowhere outside the golden realm of fancy and mythical dreaming."

On the other hand, we have the valuable testimony of contemporaneous writers who testify to what they have not only heard, but seen with their own eyes. Let us quote from two of these. Colonel Thomas Nuett Brocklehurst, a retired officer of the British army, made quite an extensive tour in Mexico in 1881. Among the points of interest visited by this observing English gentleman was Tula, and in his *Mexico To-Day* he says :

" Tula, formerly known as Tolam, was the ancient capital of the Toltec nation about the seventh century, and had necessarily a palace for its king and many temples. The palace stood on the top of a neighboring hill, and its foundation and ruins have been lately excavated by Mons. Charnay. It appears to have consisted of a great number of small rooms, narrow passages, steps, and little courts. In these latter there were, probably, from the present aspect of the ground, tanks of water. The walls were thickly plastered and painted red. Scrubby bushes and vegetation cover most of the buildings. Near the foot of the hill are the remains of two temples; the walls of the one which I visited, still standing and forming three sides of a hexagon, are twenty-five feet high and turreted, and there appears to have been a chamber or platform at about three fourths of the height, judging from a ledge and some rafter holes in the masonry. There was a large amount of stone debris round the base through which trees had forced their way and had grown up so as almost to hide the temple. Our guide said the other temple had still a perfect roof, and I made an effort to visit it; but our horses got stuck in some swampy ground, and we could not reach it.

"In the market place of Tula are four colossal pieces (one prostrate) of ancient Toltec statuary. Strange to say, the legs and feet only are standing; their height is only eight feet, and we were told they were originally brought from the palace excavated by Mons. Charnay. But what has become of the busts and heads of these monsters I was unable to find out."

That tireless traveler and lecturer of our country, Fred. A. Ober, says that Señor Cubas, in a paper, *Ruinas de la Antigua Tollam*, published in 1874, gives a list of the antiquities discovered near Tula, and lithographed figures of the most prominent sculptures, which included a "zodiac" and a "hieroglyph," now seen in the lintel of the principal entrance to the great church. In the Plaza are some great stones, taken from the ruins of the Toltec city. There are three colossal sculptures, perhaps of *caryatides*, standing erect, and another lying down. This last is in two pieces, and was formerly united by tenon and mortise, even as I found the adornments on the palace of Uxmal. Near the office of the railroad superintendent is a great stone ring, like those found in the ruins of Chichen-Itza. At the door of the cathedral is a beautiful baptismal font—at least, that is its use now—taken from these same Toltec ruins. Doubtless nearly all the buildings here were made from stone taken from the Toltec city, as you may find sculptured stones used for the pavement of courts, inserted in walls, etc.

I have thus roughly sketched the old city at which the great railroad arrived in April, 1881. Let tourists and archæologists visit it, now that they can do so with little fatigue. It does not need a more prophetic eye than belongs to ordinary man to discern the result of the opening of a country so rich in mineral and archæological wealth. For a thousand years man has lived in this country

—a thousand that are chronicled, and no one knows how many previously. The works of his hands lie scattered throughout valley and plain, crest many a hill, and adorn many a secluded vale. The time is coming when it is possible to reach many hitherto hidden from the world; daily workmen are unearthing some relic of the past, and if our scientific societies would keep pace with the development of this country they should appoint a small party of qualified men to travel over this road with the advanced engineers.

Let our American authors visit and investigate for themselves such ruins as Tula, Teotihuacan, Xochicalco, Papantla, Cholula, Mitla, Mayapan, Ake, Chichen-Itza, Xabali, Labria, Uxmal, Palenque, Xibalba, and many others less noted, but which the future may prove to be equally interesting and important, ere they push aside all tradition and sculpture testimony with a flourish of their pen. The views of many will be modified, the field of all students of history enlarged, while the world, especially in coming generations, will be made wiser by the entrance of every honest and patient investigator into this very broad and exceedingly rich field. We are very glad to lean upon others for such help from these sources, as we have neither the time nor the fitness for the necessary original

SOURCES OF INFORMATION. 23

search. Due to the patient perseverance of not a few in studying these picture paintings and the traditions of the natives, we have had access, in the preparation of these lectures, to such valuable works as the following:

1. Four voluminous letters written by the famous conqueror, Ferdinand Cortez, to Charles V, King of Spain, in which he gives his own account of the conquest, and much valuable information concerning primitive Mexico and the Mexicans. These letters were published in Spanish, Latin, Tuscan, and other languages of Europe, the first copies appearing in Seville in 1522.

2. Bernal Diaz, one of Cortez's soldiers, wrote a book entitled *Historia Verdadera de la Conquista de Nueva España*, which was published in Madrid in 1632. Though only a soldier, he proved to be quite an historian, especially in the eyes of the Church in whose interests he wrote. His success in making the Mexican side of his picture as dark as possible and glorifying the part which the "Holy Catholic Church" took in the conquest is certainly remarkable. This work has been reproduced several times in various languages.

3. "The Anonymous Conqueror" is the name given to the author of a brief but interesting work called *Relatione d'Accone cose della Nuova Spagna*, etc. (the report of a gentleman who attended Ferdinand Cortez). He confines himself chiefly to the manners and customs of the people, their temples and antiquities.

4. *La Historia de los Indios de Nueva España*, by Motolinia, his real name being Toribio de Benavente. He was one of the first twelve Franciscan monks to preach the Gospel to the natives, by whom he was given the Mexican name of Motolinia. He explains their ancient religious customs, etc. This is an exceedingly rare book, but it is quoted extensively by Mexican authors and a few American authors of modern times.

5. Bernardino de Sahagun in the sixteenth century wrote *Historia General de las Casas de Nueva Espana*, and his three volumes were reproduced in Mexico in 1829. He also wrote twelve large volumes concerning the Mexican language, the geography, the religion, the political and natural history of the Mexicans. He was a Franciscan, and devoted fifty years of his life to preaching and teaching among the natives.

6. José de Acosta, a Jesuit father, published a work of great literary merit in Seville in 1589. It was entitled *Historia Natural y Moral de las Indias*. It was reproduced in Barcelona in 1591, in French, at Paris, in 1600, and afterward, I understand, in other languages of Europe.

7. Fernando de Alva Ixtlilxochitl was a noble Indian of Tezcoco and a direct descendant of Coanacotzin, last king of Acolhuacan. By request of the viceroy he wrote four valuable works: 1. *Historia de Nueva España;* 2. *Historia Chichimeca;* 3. *Historia del Reino de Tezcoco;* and 4. *La Historia de los Toltecos*, etc. Don Fernando had the advantage of having followed other historians in his own family who had scrupulously guarded and carefully studied a full collection of picture paintings.

8. Bartolomé de Las Casas, a Dominican and first bishop of Chiapas, was, perhaps, the best friend which the Indians had among the early Spanish missionaries. He published his first work in 1552, in which he complains bitterly of Spanish cruelty to the Indians and throws much light on the ancient history of the country. This and others of his later works were published in several languages of Europe, in some cases as a matter of hatred to the Spaniards. It is to be regretted that some valuable manuscripts by this same author, one of which is said to contain 830 pages, should have been hidden under the dust of ages in old libraries of Valladolid, Madrid, and Amsterdam. If ever given to the world they will, perhaps, throw additional light on the Indian question of Chiapas and Guatemala.

9. Antonio de Herrera wrote *Historia General de los*

SOURCES OF INFORMATION. 25

Hechos de los Castellanos, etc., giving eight decades of American history beginning from the year 1492, first printed in Madrid, 1601, and afterward republished in different langages and places of the continent. Señor Herrera has the credit of being both candid and judicious. In ancient history he follows Acosta and Gomara, about 1614.

10. Juan de Torquemada, a Franciscan Spaniard, published his *Monarquia Indiana* in Madrid, in three great folio volumes. It is considered by all the most complete, up to its date, on the antiquity of Mexico. Torquemada went, when a mere youth, to the country, learned the indigenous languages, lived nearly fifty years among the Indians, and after collecting a large number of ancient pictures and manuscripts devoted some twenty years to the preparation of his work.

11. Carlos de Siguenza é Gongora, professor of mathematics in the University of Mexico in the latter part of the seventeenth century, made a large and choice collection of ancient pictures and manuscripts, and applied himself with great diligence to the antiquity of his country. In his *Mexican Cyclography* he adjusted their ancient epochs to ours, and explained the method they used to count centuries, years, and months. In his *History of the Chichimecan Empire* he explained the migration of the first colonists from Asia to America, and leading events of the most ancient nations of Anahuac. In his lengthy discourse on the *Gospel in Anahuac*, he declared his belief that St. Thomas was the first to bring the " glad tidings " to the Indians of Mexico. He bases this belief on tradition and the existence of the cross in so many parts of the country prior to the coming of the Spaniards.

The finding of the cross on this continent has given rise to great differences of opinion. Some believe it, as did all Spanish authors at and since the time of the conquest, as an evidence of the preaching of Christianity in remote times, and that the Gospel became mixed with the indigenous rites of the country. Others, however, consider it as an astronomical sign or an indication of the four points of the compass or the four seasons of the year. Others, again, say it is a figure as familiar as the Greek cross in the Old World. It is a well-known fact that the cross has been an object of worship among ancient peoples before the birth of Christ. In Egypt, in China, in Tartary, among the Druids and among the Goths we find the cross. Hence its existence does not necessarily imply the preaching of the Gospel. On this continent it was found in Canada, in Peru, on the island of Cozumel, in New Granada, in Palenque, in Brazil, in Paraguay, and in Teotihuacan—places so scattered over the continent as to make it quite improbable, if not impossible, that some Christian Quetzalcoatl introduced them into all these places.

Then, again, the cross found in ancient Mexican ruins is *not* the Latin cross, for it generally has the four arms equal in size, like the Greek cross, though sometimes as an astronomical sign they seem to follow the shape of the St. Andrew cross (x). Besides this, as Chavero remarks (in *Mexico Á Traves de los Siglos*, p. 379), attention should be fixed on this fact: the Christian religion differs from all others in having the cross as a symbol of redemption, or the symbol of a crucified Saviour for the salvation of man. But the Mexicans neither had the crucifix nor was the cross in any sense a sign of redemption, although at times it was doubtless worshiped as a deity, and at other times it was simply a symbol in chronology.

In his *Genealogy of Mexican Kings*, Siguenza established an unbroken line back to the seventh century. Unfortunately these and other important productions were never printed, and the manuscripts were lost through the negligence of his heirs. In contemporaneous writers, notably Gemelli, Betancourt, and Florencia, we find preserved many extracts from this learned professor.

12. An enterprising Italian, from Milan, by the name of Lorenzo Benaduci Boturini, reached Mexico in 1736. For eight years he made most diligent search into its antiquity. He studied the indigenous languages, lived among the Indians, obtained many of their ancient pictures and copies of their old

SOURCES OF INFORMATION. 27

manuscripts. His collection of such was second only to that of Siguenza. When, however, he was about ready to begin the writing of his History his entire literary estate was confiscated by the colonial government. On his return to Europe, and relying largely upon his memory, he published (Madrid, 1746) an outline of his contemplated History. This skeleton makes the student of Mexican history deeply deplore the atrocious conduct of the Spanish viceroy.

Besides these and many other Spanish and Mexican authors there are several anonymous works in Mexican languages on the Toltecs and Aztecs, with historic matter bearing on their languages, pilgrimages, wars, and other events, from the early part of the eleventh well down into the sixteenth century. To these might be added a long list of French, English, Italian, Dutch, Flemish, and German writers, from whom our more modern authors have been able to draw.

13. *The Travels of Thomas Gage* were published in Paris in 1625. At an early age, on account of political disturbances in Great Britain, he was sent to Spain for his education, after which he became a Dominican, and was sent as a missionary to the New World. His travels are very interesting reading, and in some cases his plain manner of speaking the truth concerning the corrupt lives of the priests in Mexico has brought upon him the criticism of more careful Church authors. Possibly this is the reason why Clavigero does not like him. We shall, however, have occasion to refer to him frequently.

14. Notwithstanding the mistakes of Dr. William Robertson, already referred to, and Clavigero's severe strictures on him, we cannot refrain from recommending his *History of America*, published in London in 1777, from which we have received no inconsiderable aid.

15. Perhaps the most popular of all works, prior to the present century, and certainly the one most frequently quoted by modern authors, is the *History of Mexico*, by the Jesuit, Francisco Javier Clavigero. This well-known Mexican writer was born in the Port of Vera Cruz in 1731 (not in 1720, as

most American encyclopedias have it). His parents were Spaniards of royal blood, and his cousin one of Mexico's rulers of the eighteenth century. He entered the Jesuit College at Puebla when only seventeen years of age, and after a course in philosophy and theology studied Greek and Hebrew under a German Jesuit. Later he acquired a mastery of Mexicano, Otomí, and Misteco, besides some knowledge of twenty other indigenous languages of the country. He lived among the Indians for thirty-six years, and became familiar with all their traditions and a ready interpreter. Together with all Spanish Jesuits he was expatriated in 1767, at which time he went to reside in Italy. Here he continued his study of Mexican history, obtaining access through brothers of the order to all the more important libraries of Europe. His work was first written in Spanish, but for political reasons which made its publication impossible in Spain he was obliged to translate it into Italian, and the first published edition of his work appeared in Bologna, 1780. It was soon after published in French, German, and English. The year of his death, 1787, the first English edition appeared in London, and in 1806 another English edition was printed in Richmond, Va. No library on Mexico is complete without this work in some one of the languages in which it has appeared, and we shall have occasion to quote frequently from this source.

16. Baron Friedrich Heinrich Alexander Von Humboldt, one of the greatest naturalists of modern times, after extensive scientific explorations on the continent, was sent by his government on a similar errand to the north of Asia. Later he went to South America, and in 1803 to Mexico. Though he only visited such points as were of easy access from the capital, he nevertheless so improved and utilized the labors of others that the whole territory bears the impress of his mighty mind. His work, *A Political Essay on the Kingdom of New Spain*, though now chiefly useful as giving statistical information regarding the country previous to and at the period of his visit, must be taken, as a later writer truly says, as the *point*

SOURCES OF INFORMATION. 29

d'appui for the works of all travelers coming after him. Though perhaps he did not discover here much that was new, or throw additional light on the history of the people, he yet brought afresh to the notice of the world the writings of the old historians, revived an interest in archæology, and set before all Europe the great natural resources of a country then inhabited by an oppressed people. His books have been a mine of wealth for subsequent historians, and have indeed served not only for reference, but as a very material portion of their productions. Besides the *Political Essay* above referred to (published in Paris, 1811, in two folio volumes), his *Geography of the New Continent (Examen Critique de l'histoire de la Geographie du Nouveau Continent)*, in five volumes, was completed in Paris in 1839. Both these and other works of this master pen have been translated and published in London and New York. His residence in Mexico was only for one short year, and yet such was the impression made by his visit, and such the high regard in which he is still held, that the city government of the capital recently marked the front of the house where he resided with an elegantly inscribed tablet. A five minutes' walk from the headquarters of the Methodist Mission takes one to the spot.

17. Our great American historian, William H. Prescott, first published his flowery *History of the Conquest of Mexico* in 1843. Within a year the entire work was reproduced in Spanish in the city of Mexico, with valuable annotations by Lucas Alaman. Another Mexican edition followed later with notes by Dr. Ramirez. Both of these writers try to correct some of the mistakes of Prescott. Few historians have made more interesting reading than Prescott, but he was a nonresident historian and depended chiefly on such books and manuscripts as had run the gauntlet of State and Church criticism in Spain during the sixteenth and seventeenth centuries. Nevertheless, no one can afford to pass by this work.

18. Lord Kingsborough's *Antiquities of Mexico*, in nine monumental folio volumes, was published in London between

1831 and 1848. This is the most beautiful and extensively illustrated work extant on Mexico, but its price, £100, puts it beyond the reach of the public in general. Only three copies exist in Mexico. In this country there is one copy at the Smithsonian Institution, another in the Bancroft Library, and, doubtless, a few other copies of which the lecturer knows not. The entire edition consisted of only five hundred copies, and is now out of print.

19. In our own times the exhaustive work of Hubert Howe Bancroft, of San Francisco, takes the lead. Mr. Bancroft has probably the largest and most valuable library on Mexican and cognate subjects in existence. His agents in America and Europe have expended over a million and a half of dollars in the collection of some three thousand book volumes, in print and manuscripts, about ten thousand pamphlets, and files of official newspapers without number. In the Preface of his first volume this voluminous author says: "I have all the standard histories and printed chronicles of the earliest times, together with all the works of writers who have extended their investigations to the events and developments of later years. On the shelves of my library are found the various *Colecciones de Documentos*, filled with precious historical papers from the Spanish and Mexican archives, all that were consulted in manuscript by Robertson, Prescott, and other able writers, with thousands equally important that were unknown to them. My store of manuscript material is rich both in originals and copies, including the treasures secured during a long experience by such collectors as José Maria Andrade and José Fernando Ramirez; a copy of the famous *Archivo General de Mexico*, in thirty-two volumes; the autograph originals of Carlos Maria Bustamente's historical writings, in about fifty volumes, containing much not found in his printed works; the original records of the earliest Mexican councils of the Church, with many ecclesiastical and missionary chronicles not extant in print; and, finally, a large amount of copies of material on special topics drawn from different archives expressly for my

SOURCES OF INFORMATION. 31

work." Mexico is but one part of the great American question treated by Mr. Bancroft, and the fourteen large volumes which we possess are but a fraction of his extensive work. He certainly deserves due credit for his immense research, whatever may be the opinion of critical judges on his painstaking and thoroughness. It is a marvel to us how any one man could produce so much in a single lifetime.

20. A lamented friend, graduate of Drew Theological Seminary, and, later, professor in the Ohio State University, John T. Short, published in 1880 (Harper Brothers) *The North Americans of Antiquity*, which gives valuable information on one phase of our subject.

21. *Life in Mexico*, published in Boston in 1843 by Madame Calderon de la Barca, wife of the first Spanish ambassador to Mexico, after the mother country recognized the latter's independence, as the title implies, throws much light on another phase of the subject, and is regarded as a most admirable portraiture of Mexican domestic habits and customs.

22. Brantz Mayer, at one time secretary of the American legation in Mexico, published between 1843 and 1853 four different works, of which the most valuable is *Mexico: Aztec, Spanish, and Republican*, which appeared in 1850 and covers the period of the Mexican war.

23. Dr. Gorham D. Abbott, principal of the Springler Institute, New York, made a study of the Great Question of the Western Hemisphere, in contradistinction to the Great Eastern Question, at that time agitating all Europe, for the transit of the commerce of Asia between the Mediterranean and the Persian Gulf, and, as a result, published his *Mexico and the United States*, in 1869. His book is an important contribution to the political and military history of the country, especially from 1824 to 1859.

24. In 1846 the Hon. Waddy Thompson, after a term of service as United States minister, published his *Recollections of Mexico*. His strictures on what he is pleased to call the " disgusting mummeries and impostures " of the Roman

Catholic Church, "which degrade the Christian religion into an absurd, ridiculous, and venal superstition," are almost as true to-day as they were forty-five years ago. But his southern depreciation of "the poor and motherless black Indian" would doubtless undergo a change if he could have seen Benito Juarez, a pure Indian, rising up as the human saviour of Mexico's millions from the degradation of that "absurd, ridiculous, and venal superstition."

25. In 1855 to 1856 and 1859 Robert A. Wilson published three different works. The last, entitled *Mexico: Its Peasants and Its Priests*, is, perhaps, the most interesting.

More recent publications are numerous, and we have only time to mention Frost's *Pictorial History of Mexico and the Mexican War* (Richmond, 1848); *Our Sister Republic*, Albert S. Evans (Hartford, 1870); *Our Next-Door Neighbor*, by the lamented Gilbert Haven (Harpers, 1875); *Travels in Mexico* (Boston, 1883), F. A. Ober; *Mexico To-day*, Thomas Nuett Brocklehurst (London, 1883); *Native Religions of Mexico and Peru* (Scribner, 1884), by Dr. Albert Reville, translated by P. H. Wicksteed; *Aztec Land* (Boston, 1890), by Maturin M. Ballou; a number of valuable reports from the Bureau of American Republics, Washington, and, finally, *Mexico in Transition* (Hunt & Eaton, 1892), by Dr. William Butler. Our relation to the author forbids our saying too much of this last work, but we are authorized to quote freely from it as we proceed. The many Spanish and Mexican authors cannot be mentioned here for want of space. The field is an immense one; the resources of information are without number; we earnestly trust that wisdom may be given to so present the subject as to merit your kind attention during the few days we spend together in these classic halls of Syracuse.

LECTURE II.

ORIGIN OF THE MEXICANS.

LECTURE II.

ORIGIN OF THE MEXICANS.

NOT less than sixteen distinct theories are advocated concerning the origin of the first inhabitants of this western continent. "From whence did they come?" has been asked again and again, and received many different answers.

The theory claiming an autochthonic origin for these most ancient inhabitants has had able ethnologists among its advocates. But with Mr. Bancroft, who had carefully studied all published arguments, we agree that to express belief in a theory incapable of proof appears to be idle. "Indeed, such belief is not belief; it is merely acquiescing in or accepting a hypothesis or tradition until the contrary is proved."* Those who advocate this theory are of two classes, evolutionists and believers in separate, multiplied creations, this latter class claiming as many Adams and Eves as there are different species of the human genera. Some of this school, however, in advancing this theory hasten to add: "We do not at all derogate from God's greatness,

* *Native Races*, vol. v, p. 131.

nor in any way dishonor the sacred evidence given us by his servants."

The antiquity of the American race seems to have induced many to accept one of the above leadings.

Professor John T. Short well says: "We have seen that as yet no truly scientific proof of man's great antiquity in America exists. This conclusion is concurred in by most eminent authorities. At present we are probably not warranted in claiming for him a much longer residence on this continent than that assigned him by Sir John Lubbock, namely, three thousand years. Future research may develop the fact that man is as old here as in Europe, and that he was contemporaneous with the mastodon. As the case stands in the present state of knowledge it furnishes strong presumptive evidence that man is not autochthonic here, but exotic, having originated in the Old World, perhaps thousands of years prior to reaching the New."

Professor Joseph Henry, in *Smithsonian Report*, 1866, expresses himself as follows:

"The spontaneous generation of either plants or animals, although a legitimate subject of scientific inquiry, is as yet an unverified hypothesis. If, however, we assume the fact that a living being will be spontaneously produced when all the physical con-

ORIGIN OF THE MEXICANS. 37

ditions necessary to its existence are present, we must allow that in the case of man, with his complex and refined organization, the fortuitous assembly of the multiform conditions required for his appearance would be extremely rare, and from the doctrine of probabilities could scarcely occur more than at one time and in one place on our planet; and further, that this place would most probably be somewhere in the northern temperate zone. Again, the Caucasian variety of man presents the highest physical development of the human family; and as we depart either to the north or south, from the latitude assumed as the origin of the human race in Asia, we meet with a lower type, until at the north we encounter the Eskimos, and at the south the Bosjesman and the Tierra del Fuegian. The derivation of these varieties from the original stock is philosophically explained on the principle of the variety in the offspring of the same parents, and the better adaptation and consequent change of life of some of these to the new conditions of existence in a more northern or southern latitude."

The most celebrated advocate of the indigenous theory is Dr. Samuel G. Morton, of Philadelphia, who published his *Crania Americana* in 1839. His conclusions, as quoted by Short,* are (1) "That

* *North Americans of Antiquity*, p. 130.

the American race differs essentially from all others, not excepting the Mongolian;" (2) "That the American nations, excepting the polar tribes, are one race and one species;" and (3) "That the cranial remains discovered in the mounds, from Peru to Wisconsin, belong to the same race, and probably to the Toltecan family." It may be rather strained to set these crumbling crania down as Toltecan, but in view of such airy conclusions the following observations of the learned Retzins, in *Smithsonian Report* for 1859, are significant: "This author (Dr. Morton), who has given us such numerous and valuable facts, as well as the linguists who have studied these American languages with indefatigable zeal, have arrived at the conclusion that both race and language in the New World are unique. I am obliged to avow that the facts advanced by Morton himself, and that the study of numerous skulls with which he has enriched the Museum of Stockholm, have conducted me to a wholly different result. I can only explain the fact by surmising that this remarkable man has allowed the views of the naturalist to be warped by his linguistic researches." After showing how Dr. Morton's published plates contradict his theory Retzins continues: "Conclusive, however, as the plates are, I should scarcely have ventured to advance these remarks if the rich series of our own collection and the numerous and excellent figures of Blumenbach, Sandifort, Van der Hoeven, etc., did not declare in favor of my opinion."

Latham, in his *Natural History of the Varieties of Man* (p. 452), quotes Morton's tables to show the fallacy of his (Morton's) conclusions.

The color and stature arguments, so often appealed to, do not substantiate Dr. Morton's theory. Prichard, in *Researches into the Physical History of Mankind* (fourth edition, 1841, vol. i, p. 269), as quoted by Professor Short, remarks: "It will be easy to prove that the American races, instead of displaying a uniformity of color in all climates, show nearly as great a variety in this respect as the nations of the old continent; that there are among them white races with a florid complexion inhabiting temperate regions, and tribes black or of very dark hue in low and intertropical countries; that their stature, figure, and countenance are almost equally diversified." All of which is confirmed by travel and observation in Mexico alone, where one finds the Zuñi and the Pinto, the Yaqui and the Yucateco, with their marvelous dissimilarity in color and in stature.

The unparalleled diversity of language which

meets the philologist everywhere on this continent is certainly against the idea of the ethnic unity of ancient American peoples. Mr. Bancroft claims one thousand three hundred languages and dialects for the New World, and he has classified six hundred of them, thirty-seven of which are spoken in Mexico to-day.

Professor Short adds: "It is true that the American languages present a few features quite peculiar to themselves, but as language is never constant it is not a pyramid with its unchanging architectural plan, but it is a plant which passes through such transitions in the process of its growth as to lose entirely some of the elements which it possessed at first; so we may as reasonably expect that in the course of time certain peculiarities incident to certain climatic conditions, certain phases of nature, and certain types of civilization should develop themselves as distinguishing features of the speech of the continent. The very fact that language is unstable—is a matter of growth—renders the argument that these peculiarities indicate unity of the American race valueless; while, on the other hand, the fact that here we have a greater number and variety of languages than is to be found in any of the other grand divisions of the earth is strong evidence of a diversity more radical than that which simply arises from tribal affiliations. In view of the wide differences existing between the native Americans themselves, in every feature which admits of being subjected to a scientific test, we are forced to the conclusion, solely resting on the evidence in the case, that the theory of American ethnic unity is a delusion, an infatuating theory which served only to blind its advocates as to the plain facts, and led them into grave errors, which will become all the more palpable as scientific investigation progresses.

"As yet no substantial reason for considering the ancient occupant of this continent as peculiar in himself, and as unlike the rest of mankind, has been set forth. Nothing in the American's physical organization points to an origin different from that to which each of the species of the *genus homo* may be assigned. Whatever truth there may be in the diverse origin of the black and white races, the separate creation theory, in so far as it maintains that the Creator originated upon the soil of this continent a peculiar and separate race of men, must, in the eyes of this age of criticism, lack evidence and be assigned to its place with thousands of others which from time immemorial have been contributing to the construction of a foundation reef which will ultimately rise like a bold headland above the dark waters of uncertainty into the realm of truth."

Even Mr. Darwin (in *Descent of Man*, vol. i, p. 188) and Professor Haeckel, than whom there could be no more celebrated representatives of the development school, object decidedly to the theory of the autochthonic origin of the ancient American families. And Mr. H. Tuttle, in *Origin and Antiquity of Physical Man Scientifically Considered*, says: "If a species or variety of the *genus homo* sprang up in Europe and another in America by agency of conditions existing in these localities, it would be beyond probability that they should both be formed on the same plan."

Baron Humboldt thinks that not only the Red Indians, but the Toltecs and Aztecs also, were of Asiatic origin.* And Mr. Tylor, in *Anahuac* (London, 1861, p. 104), says: "On the whole, the most probable view of the origin of the Mexican tribes seems to be the one ordinarily held, that they really came from the Old World, bringing with them several legends, evidently the same as the histories recorded in the Book of Genesis."

It seems to us, in common with Professor Short, that there is nothing to indicate that the primitive "Americans owe their origin to a special act of

* *Essai Polit.*, vol. i, p. 79, Paris, 1811.

creation." Indeed, the best of writers on American ethnology and antiquities not only reject this " special creation " theory, but also the theory of evolution, declaring "if they originated by the process of development (for which there is no sufficient evidence) that it was not upon the American continent."

To our mind there is no doubt involving the Old World origin of the Americans. From whence they came or to what particular people or peoples they owed their birth we may not be able clearly to determine, but we may at least study the question with great interest, and we believe with profit, too, reaching, perhaps, the same conclusion that Professor Short did, namely, " That view seems open to least objections which maintains that the western continent received its population at a comparatively early period in the history of the race, before the peoples of western Europe and eastern Asia had assumed their present national characteristics or fully developed their religious and social customs."* This is also the opinion of most Mexican authors. Señor Ezequiel Uricoechea thus expresses their commonly accepted view : " Hence remaining to us one primordial origin for all the human race, then the question is to

* *The North Americans of Antiquity*, p. 202.

know from what trunk or family of the old continent the new was populated, or even *vice versa*, which is also possible, though improbable, that from what we call the new the old continent was populated."* This last is a daring leap in conjecture.

As stated above, we have found in our study of the question sixteen different theories touching the origin of the primitive Americans. These may be divided into three classes, and for convenience' sake we designate them the European, the African, and the Asiatic theories.

Of the European theories there are six:

1. The Welsh theory. We have a neighbor in the city of Mexico whose hair fairly bristles and whose eyes dance with delight whenever he dilates on the fact that before Edward I perfected the union of Wales and England, begun by William the Conqueror, in 1170 A. D., an illustrious Welshman led a number of his countrymen across the great and then unknown Atlantic and discovered America.

This pre-Columbian sailor was named Madoc-Ap-owen, and a full account of his first and second transatlantic voyages is found in old Welsh annals, a translation of which was published in 1589.

The story in substance is this: Madoc was one

* *Soc. Mex. Bol.*, second edition, vol. iv, p. 128, 1854.

ORIGIN OF THE MEXICANS. . 45

of several sons born to Owen Gwynedd, Prince of North Wales. After the father's death the sons contended violently for rulership. Madoc, being of a peaceful disposition, determined to sail for some unknown country where he might dwell in quietness. For many months he and his handful of followers sailed westward without finding a resting place, "but at length they came to a large and fertile country." The annals also state that Madoc and a part of his men returned after a while to Wales, and induced a large number of their countrymen to join them in their second voyage to America. It is supposed that they, with their ten ships, reached the colony in safety, but nothing more is said about them in these Celtic annals.

The exact locality of the colony is still a disputed question. Baldwin says, "Somewhere in the Carolinas." But a noted Welsh historian, Caradoc, insists that the colony was established in Mexico, and gives three reasons: First, the Mexicans believed that their ancestors came from a beautiful country inhabited by white people, witness Quetzalcoatl; secondly, they adored the cross, witness Palenque; and, thirdly, that Welsh names are found in Mexico.

Another Welsh writer says: "Moctezuma, King, or rather Emperour, of Mexico, did recount unto the Spaniards, at their first coming, that his ancestors came from a farre countrie, and were white people. Which, conferred with an ancient chronicle, that I have read many years since, may be conjectured to be a Prince of Wales, who many hundreth years since, with certaine shippes, sayled to the westwards, with intent to make new discoveries."*

Some claim that the aborigines of Virginia and of Guatemala celebrated the memory of an ancient hero called Madoc; others say that he came through the Gulf of Mexico and up the Mississippi till he settled on the banks of the Ohio. There are reports that traces of the Welsh colony and of their language are found among native tribes in different parts of the United States. Bancroft, in *Native Races* (vol. v, p. 119), publishes a curious letter, written by the Rev. Morgan Jones in 1686, in which he claims that when he fell into the hands of the Tuscarora tribe he and his five companions were about to be put to death, when he soliloquized aloud in Welsh; whereupon their lives were spared.

Lieutenant Roberts states that in 1801 an Indian chief who spoke Welsh fluently came to Washington. He claimed that there was a tradition among his people that his ancestors came "from a distant country, which lay far to the east, over the great waters." The children of this tribe were not

* Hawkins Voy. in Hakluyt Soc., p. 111.

ORIGIN OF THE MEXICANS. 47

allowed to learn any other tongue till they were twelve years of age. About forty years ago two eminent Welshmen traveling and studying in America " collected upwards of one hundred different accounts of Welsh Indians."

2. The Irish theory carries us back to the fifth century, when, it is claimed, St. Patrick preached the Gospel in the "isles of America" and an Irish colony was established along the coast from North Carolina to Florida, called "White Man's Land," from whence some passed on to Mexico. But, as it was claimed that " White Man's Land " was only " six days' sail from Ireland," and the word " America " is found in the story at that early date, Professor Short is doubtless correct in saying that the claim " carries its own refutation upon its face."

After a residence of twenty years in the country there is only one evidence which we have met that might be considered as favoring the Irish theory, and even this must be considered in the light of a modern *tradition*.

From the early days of the present century down to 1876 history records an almost uninterrupted series of disturbances in Mexico. Sometimes on the slightest pretext people were up in arms against the existing government.

Now, there is a modern *tradition* that a newly

arrived emigrant from Hibernia, on being informed, in reply to his first question at Castle Garden, that there was a government, declared with his accustomed patriotism, " *Well, then, I'm agin the government.*" How many of these oft-repeated revolutions are due to the existence of Irish blood in Mexican veins we do not pretend to say.

3. The Scotch theory is based upon the assertions of a gentleman from the Highlands of Scotland finding Indian tribes in Florida whose languages "had the greatest affinity with the Celtic in their speech." We are assured, too, that "the Indian names of several of the streams, brooks, mountains, and rocks of Florida are also the same which are given to similar objects in the Highlands of Scotland."*

Lord Monboddo, writing in the seventeenth century, gives several instances to prove that the language of the native Highlanders was found in America, and that an Eskimo could readily converse with a Scotchman after only a few days' practice.

4. Not a few authors believe that the Americans descended from the ancient inhabitants of the Grecian Archipelago. George Jones, in his *History of Ancient America* (London, 1843), believes that the

* Priest's *American Antiquities*, p. 230.

ORIGIN OF THE MEXICANS. 49

sculpture of ruins in Uxmal, Yucatan, follow the Greek style.

Brasseur de Bourbourg claims identity between some American gods and Greek deities. Mons. Lafitau, in *Mœurs des Sauvages Ameriquains Comparées aux Mœurs des Premiers Temps* (Paris, 1724), says that the subjects of Og, King of Bashan, drove ancient Greeks from their home, and he thinks he finds them in America. Idolatry, the use of sacred fire, bacchanalian revels, resemblances in marriage customs, system of education, manner of hunting, fishing, and making war, games and sports, treatment of the sick, mourning and burial customs, are all quoted to support his view.

Another writer reports hearing of a rock in Peru containing something which looked like a Greek inscription.

William Pidgeon, in *Traditions of Decoodah, and Antiquarian Researches* (New York, 1858), says that a farmer in Brazil discovered, in 1827, " a flat stone, upon which was engraved a Greek inscription which, as far as it was legible, read as follows : ' During the dominion of Alexander, the son of Philip, King of Macedon, in the sixty-third Olympiad, Ptolemaios.' Deposited beneath the stone were found two ancient swords, a helmet, and a shield. On the handle of one of the swords was a portrait of Alexander ; on the helmet was a beautiful design representing Achilles dragging the corpse of Hector round the walls of Troy." Mr. Pidgeon draws the conclusion "that the soil of Brazil was formerly broken by Ptolemaios, more than a thousand years before the discovery of Columbus." *

5. The Roman theory rests on the vastness of certain ruins, the remains of fine roads, the fondness of ancient Americans for gladiatorial combats, and a few coins reported to have been found at different places on the continent. Priest, Torquemada, Villagutierre, and Lord Kingsborough give more or less credit to these evidences.

6. The Norseman theory seems well established, and, while it does not go so far back as several of the others, it does antedate by nearly five hundred years the coming of Columbus. Baron Humboldt sums up the evidence thus: " The discovery of the northern part of America by the Northmen cannot be disputed. The length of the voyage, the direction in which they sailed, the time of the sun's rising and setting, are accurately given. While the caliphate of Bagdad was still flourishing under the Abbassides, and while the rule of the Samoieds, so favorable to poetry, still flourished in Persia, America was discovered about the year 1000 by

* *Native Races*, vol. v, p. 123.

ORIGIN OF THE MEXICANS. 51

Lief, son of Eric the Red, at about 41 1-2° north latitude."

The publication of original documents by the Royal Society at Copenhagen ought to be sufficient to satisfy the most skeptical. Mr. B. F. De Costa says there can be no doubt as to their authenticity, and Hubert Howe Bancroft agrees with him, though George Bancroft and Washington Irving do not; but the latter frankly confesses that he did not have the "means of tracing this story to its original sources."

Mr. George Bancroft disposes of the entire subject in one page, while his later and more persistent namesake devotes the good part of a chapter to the subject in the light of these original documents published at Copenhagen. His entire first chapter on this general subject in *Native Races*, vol. v, is most interesting. Part of it is quite romantic.

Mr. R. B. Anderson, who published *America Not Discovered by Columbus* (Chicago, 1874), claims that the Northmen left a greater impression upon Americans than is generally believed.

M. Grarier, in his *Discovery of America by Norsemen* (Paris, 1864), attributes Aztec civilization to Norse influence. The famous Abbé Brasseur de Bourbourg is quoted as agreeing with them. He claims to have found many words in the languages of Central America with marked Scandinavian traces, also ancient traditions which point to a northeast origin. This Norse influence is frequently referred to by contemporaneous authors in Mexico.

Of the African theories there are four:

1. The Egyptian theory seems based entirely upon analogies. These analogies are said "to exist between the architecture, hieroglyphics, methods of computing time, and, to a less extent, customs of the two countries."*

Carlos Siguenza y Gorgora, writing in the latter part of the seventeenth century, believed that the posterity of Naphtuhim "left Egypt not long after the confusion of tongues and traveled toward America." Pierre Daniel Huet, a noted French bishop of the early part of the eighteenth century, accepts Siguenza's conclusions, and, in addition to the above reasons, adds "the resemblance of the word *Teotl* of the Mexicans to the *Theuth* of the Egyptians."

Concerning archæological analogies, Garcia Cubas gives the following between the pyramids of San Juan Teotihuacan (only twenty miles from the city of Mexico) and those of Egypt: "The site chosen is the same; the structures are *oriented* with slight

* *Native Races*, vol. v, p. 55.

ORIGIN OF THE MEXICANS. 53

variations; the line through the center of the pyramids is the astronomical meridian; the construction in grades and steps is the same; in both cases the larger pyramids are dedicated to the sun; the Nile has a 'valley of the dead,' and at Teotihuacan there is a 'street of the dead;' some monuments of each class have the nature of fortifications; the smaller mounds are of the same nature and same purposes; both pyramids have a small mound joined to one of their faces; the openings found in the Pyramid of the Moon are also found in some Egyptian pyramids; the interior arrangement is analogous."*

Clavigero does not see so much in the pyramidal analogy as in the matter of computing time. On this point he says: "In the mode of computing time the Mexicans were much more similar to the Egyptians. . . . The Egyptian solar year was composed of three hundred and sixty-five days, like that of the Mexicans; the one and the other contained three hundred and sixty-five days in their years, and as the Egyptians added five days to their last month, *Mesori*, so did the Mexicans to their month *Izcalli*, in which particular they agreed with the Persians."

In the matter of hieroglyphics he adds: "Many

* *Ensayo de un Estudio Comparativo*, Garcia Cubas, Mexico.
5

other nations have done the same to conceal the mysteries of their religions."

The manner of dress is another argument. In Gen. x (as well as 1 Chron. i) we read that Naphtuhim was the third son of Mizraim (verse 13), who was the second son of Ham (verse 6), who in turn was the second son of Noah (verse 1). Smith's *Bible Dictionary* locates the tribe of Naphtuhim in Egypt, and says that they are spoken of in the Egyptian inscriptions "in a general manner when the kings are said, in laudatory inscriptions, *to have subdued great nations*, such as the Negroes, or extensive countries, such as Keesh, or Cush" (vol. ii. p. 463).

Kitto, however, identifies "Naphtuhim with the city of Naphata or Napata, the capital of an ancient Ethiopian kingdom, and one of the most splendid cities in Africa." He also thinks Naphtuhim, or Napata, was the royal seat of Queen Candace, mentioned in connection with the baptism of the eunuch by Philip, and thereby makes, to say the least, a very curious connection between one of the ancient tribes of the Old Testament and an incident in apostolic times (Acts viii, 27; see also McClintock & Strong, vol. vi, p. 844). Villagutierre, Orrio, and Torquemada all believe that Ham was the father of the American race, though the

ORIGIN OF THE MEXICANS.

former believes that his descendants came by land.*

2. The Carthaginian theory seems to be based on tradition, in support of which the fact of their knowledge of, and fondness for, navigation is much quoted.

Hamro, a Carthaginian navigator, is reported by several ancient authors to have made wonderful voyages of discovery, and some modern writers think that he came as far as the American continent and planted a colony.

This story is very much mixed, by some authors, with the Phœnician story, which we will consider in connection with Asiatic theories. But this confusion is not so strange when we remember that Carthage was itself a colony of Phœnicia and evidently one of its most important possessions. Its commanding position on the Mediterranean, about where the modern Tunis now stands, was duly appreciated by this maritime-loving people. Hence in time it became a great commercial and warlike republic till its dispute of the empire of the world with Rome gave rise to the famous Punic wars. It is chiefly the extended power of this African republic that leads many to give importance to certain analogies between ancient Mexican tribes and the Carthaginians.

* *Native Races*, vol. v, p. 11.

3. On the northwestern corner of Africa was founded the ancient empire of Numidia, with its twelve hundred miles of coast line. It was at one time distinguished for prosperity, population, and wealth.

"It was one of the chief granaries of Rome, and was second only to Egypt in fertility. The Roman writers called it the soul of the republic and the jewel of the empire. . . . Many wild beasts were sent hence to Rome to be exhibited in its amphitheaters." *

Tradition, especially among early Church authors of Spanish origin, says that the Numidians sailed west as well as east; that they went far beyond the Canary Islands till they came to a great island and established colonies in what is now Mexican territory.

4. The Atlantis theory. Twenty-five years ago the mere mention of this theory provoked a smile. But of late writers are giving it most thoughtful attention. We prefer to mention it in connection with the African theories because it seems to us that the weight of evidence is in favor of Afric-American connection rather than any other continuous land connection on the Atlantic side. We are aware that that Nestor of Methodist college

---

* Mitchell's *Ancient Geography*, p. 65.

ORIGIN OF THE MEXICANS. 57

presidents, Dr. W. F. Warren, in *Paradise Found* (p. 186), locates the lost Atlantis in the Paleo-Arctic Ocean. But while, as in other days, we would gladly sit at his feet to learn, we can but feel the force of the theory of the mid-Atlantic location of this supposed continent, especially in the light of recent naval explorations conducted by the British, German, and American governments severally.

The story of Atlantis as translated from Plato, in his *Timæus*, and published in Foster's *Prehistoric Races* (p. 394); in Bancroft's *Native Races* (vol. v, p. 123); in Clavigero's *History of Mexico;* in Chavero, *A Traves de los Siglos* (vol. i, p. 64), and others, is as follows:

"Among the great deeds of Athens, of which recollection is preserved in our books, there is one which should be placed above all others. Our books tell us that the Athenians destroyed an army which came across the Atlantic Sea and insolently invaded Europe and Asia, for this sea was then navigable, and beyond the strait where you place the Pillars of Hercules there was an island larger than Asia (Minor) and Libya combined. From this island one could pass easily to other islands, and from these to the continent which lies around the interior sea. The sea on this side of the strait (the Mediterranean) of which we speak resembles a harbor with a narrow entrance; but there is a genuine sea, and the land which surrounds it is a veritable continent. In the island of Atlantis reigned three kings with great and marvelous power. They had under their dominion the whole of Atlantis, several other islands, and some parts of the continent. At one time their power extended into Libya, and into Europe as far as Tyrrhénia, and, uniting their whole force, they sought to destroy our countries at a blow; but their defeat stopped the invasion and gave entire independence to all the countries this side of the Pillars of Hercules. Afterward, in one day and one fatal night, there came mighty earthquakes and inundations which engulfed the warlike people. Atlantis disappeared beneath the sea, and then that sea became inaccessible, so that navigation on it ceased on account of the quantity of mud which the engulfed island left in its place."

Plutarch, in his *Life of Solon*, relates that when that lawgiver was in Egypt "he conferred with the priests and learned from them the story of Atlantis."

Diodorus Siculus states that, "Over against Africa lies a very great island in the vast ocean, many days' sail from Libya westward."

Dr. J. W. Foster adds: "These passages from the

ancient classics as to the existence of a western continent, coupled with certain traditions to be found in the ancient Mexican records of a great catastrophe, the combined results of earthquakes and inundations, by which a large area in Central America became submerged and a greater portion of the population destroyed, have reopened the discussion whether Plato's story of Atlantis does not belong to the sobrieties of truth." *

Mr. George Catlin, in *The Lifted and Subsided Rocks of America* (London, 1870), tells how the native tribes in Mexico and Central America, in British and Dutch Guinea, clearly describe such a cataclysm. In a volume written four years earlier he tells of such a tradition among the Indians of North America.

The most enthusiastic advocate of this story is the famous Abbé Brasseur de Bourbourg. Hubert Howe Bancroft quotes extensively from the abbé's earlier and later work on the *Codex Chimalpopoca*, and while he does not accept all his conclusions he does say, " I know no man better qualified than was Brasseur de Bourbourg to penetrate the obscurity of American primitive history. His familiarity with the Nahua and Central American languages, his indefatigable industry and general erudition,

* *Prehistoric Races*, p. 396.

rendered him eminently fit for such a task, and every word written by such a man on such a subject is entitled to respectful consideration."*

The abbé's persistent study of an ancient manuscript in the Nahua language, which he calls the *Codex Chimalpopoca*, and which purports to be a *History of the Kingdoms of Culhuacan and Mexico*, led him to the conclusion that what is now the Gulf of Mexico and the Caribbean Sea was formerly solid land, and that this land extended across the Atlantic Ocean possibly as far as the Canary Islands. He also believed that the first civilization of the earth was on the lost Atlantis, "that the first ceremonial religion commenced there, as well as the first age of bronze, which spread over the two hemispheres, and that we have the beginning and basis of American ethnology." He appeals to comparative philology to support his views:

"The word Atlas and Atlantic have no satisfactory etymology in any language known to Europe. They are not Greek, and cannot be referred to any known language of the Old World.† But in the Nahuatl (or Toltecan) language we find immediately the radical *a*, *atl*, which signifies water, man, and the top of the head. From this

---

* *Native Races*, p 127.
† *Vocab. en lengua Mexicana y Castellana*, Molina.

comes a series of words, such as *Atlan*, on the border of, or amid the water, from which we have the adjective *Atlantic*. We have also *atlaca*, to combat, or to be in agony ; it means, also, to hurl or dart from the water, and in the preterit makes *Atlaz*. A city named Atlan existed when the continent was discovered by Columbus in the Gulf of Urba, Darien, with a good harbor, but is now reduced to an unimportant pueblo named Acla." *
Charles Martins, in *Revue des Deux Mondes* (March, 1867), says that "Hydrography, geology, and botany agree in teaching us that the Azores, the Canaries, and Madeira are the remains of a great continent."

The interesting account of the voyages and explorations of the United States ship *Dolphin*, the German frigate *Gazelle*, and her majesty's ships *Lightning*, *Porcupine*, and *Challenger*, as given by Professor John T. Short (p. 501, *et seq.*), are confirmatory of Martins's first argument. On the second argument a member of the *Challenger* staff, in a lecture delivered in London soon after their return, "expressed the fullest confidence that the great submarine plateau is the remains of the 'lost Atlantis,' citing as proof the fact that the inequalities, the mountains and valleys of its surface, could never

* *Prehistoric Races*, p. 397.

have been produced in accordance with any laws for the disposition of sediment nor by submarine elevation, but, on the contrary, must have been carved by agencies acting above the water level." On the third argument it is interesting to note that Sir C. Wyville Thomson, of the same ship, says he "found that the fauna of the coast of Brazil brought up by his dredging machine were similar to that of the western coast of south Europe."

Among the most interesting objects in the National Museum of the city of Mexico is a colossal head of diorite which stands three feet high. It has long been a study for all Mexican and some foreign archæologists. It is now generally believed that Señor Eufemio Abadiano has discovered its true meaning, in declaring it to be a "personification of Atlantis, the lost continent." With the *Codex Chimalpopoca*, already referred to, in his hand, Señor Abadiano made a careful study of this curious piece of ancient sculpture. He finds the story of the great catastrophe by which Atlantis was submerged explained to his satisfaction, and puts the date of its occurrence at about 1000 B. C., at which period the great Votan, of whom we shall speak more fully later on, reached Mexico.

Edward Garcynski, at this date traveling and studying in Mexico, says, "We have only to thank

Plato for the name of the lost continent;" but, after referring to Abadiano's *Study of the Codex Chimalpopoca*, he adds, "It is in Mexican literature that we find precise statements."

In *Smithsonian Report* for 1859 (p. 266) Professor Retzins declares: "We find one and the same form of skull in the Canary Islands, in front of the African coast, and in the Carib Islands on the opposite coast, which faces Africa. . . . The color of the skin on both sides of the Atlantic is represented in these populations as being of a reddish brown. . . . These facts involuntarily recall the tradition which Plato tells us in his *Timæus* was communicated to Solon by an Egyptian priest, *representing* the ancient Atlantis."

Dr. Le Plongeon found that the sandals upon the feet of the great goddess Chaacmol, which he discovered in Yucatan, and of the statue of a priestess found on the island of Mujeres, "are exact representations of those found on the feet of the Guanches, the early inhabitants of the Canary Islands, whose mummies are yet occasionally met with in the caves of Teneriffe and the other isles of the group."

Bishop Las Casas, who devotes an entire chapter to this lost island or continent, not only expresses his firm belief in its existence, but suggests that possibly Columbus had read Plato's story, and thought, perchance, that the submerged land had left another island or continent still above the water which might reward his patience and perseverance. Count Buffon, of Burgundy, one of the most famous naturalists and writers of the eighteenth century (died in Paris, 1788), believed that Africa and America were formerly connected with this great chain of rock, whose rugged links are now buried in a waste of waters.

Siguenza, as frequently quoted by Clavigero, believed in the *Atlantida*. And Clavigero himself says: "For the reasons we have already submitted we are persuaded that there was formerly a great tract of land which united the now most eastern part of Brazil to the most western part of Africa, and that all that space of land may have been sunk by some violent earthquake." *

In 1737 Mons. de Bauche presented to the Royal Academy of Science, of Paris, hydrographical charts of that part of the Atlantic Ocean in support of this same theory. It is said that his charts "were examined and approved by the academy."

It is sometimes argued that it is inconceivable to suppose any earthquake could destroy such an immense tract of land, which, according to some, must

* *History of Mexico*, vol. iii, p. 117.

have been about one thousand five hundred miles long. But it is not necessary to insist that it was the work of one shock; it might have been a succession of shocks. It should not be forgotten that it is stated in history that in 1663 one single quake completely leveled a chain of rocky mountains three hundred miles long in Canada. No one can say what might have happened, or would even happen now, if the great masses of combustible matter in the immense natural mines under our feet should become ignited and communicate with each other. Would it require more physical force to submerge an Atlantis than to throw an Ixtaccihuatl or a Popocatepetl seventeen and nineteen thousand feet up into the air, and leave them standing there with their heads in the eternal snows while the ages come and go? Perhaps the very disappearance of the Atlantis chains under the Atlantic billows may have been succeeded by the upheaval of the Mexican volcanoes, for land and water must always carry the same proportion.

In the contemplation of such majestic facts we may sing as did Moses fifteen centuries before Christ (Deut. xxxii, 3), or the psalmist later (Psalm cxi, 2), or the aged apostle in exile on lonely Patmos, "Great and marvelous are thy works Lord God Almighty" (Rev. xv, 3).

Of the Asiatic theories there are at least six, under all of which there is, perhaps, some foundation of truth. This seems quite evident when we find, as we shall later, that several of the tribes of Mexico preserve, in their traditions and paintings, the memory of the creation, the deluge, the Tower of Babel, the confusion of tongues, and the dispersion of the people.

1. The theory found in the *Book of Mormon* hardly merits mention. The story is given in Bancroft's *Native Races*, vol. v, and covers five pages (p. 96, *et seq.*). It is rather romantic and reaches from the Tower of Babel, soon after which it is claimed the first Mormons came to this continent, down to September 22, 1827, when Joseph Smith removed the buried book from the hill of Cumorah, Ontario County, N. Y. The whole story is not only a pretentious fraud, but also a blasphemous perversion of Old Testament history.

The learned John Fiske in his recent valuable work, *The Discovery of America* (Boston, 1892), well says: "It is extremely difficult for an impostor to concoct a narrative without making blunders that can easily be detected by a critical scholar. For example, the *Book of Mormon*, in the passage cited, in supremely blissful ignorance introduces oxen, sheep, and silkworms, as well as the knowledge of

ORIGIN OF THE MEXICANS. 67

smelting iron, into pre-Columbian America" (vol. i, p. 179).

2. The Jewish theory. Probably no theory has given origin to greater discussion than that the lost tribes of Israel were the first populators of all the Pacific States as far south as Peru. Learned men are found arrayed on both sides of the question.

Father Diego Duran, of vast erudition in the ancient history of Mexico, is the first author of note to publish this plan. He wrote in 1585. From a study of traditions and picture painting, aided by an aged Indian at Cholula, who had lived nearly a hundred years, he came to the "conclusion that these natives are of the ten tribes of Israel that Shalmaneser, king of the Assyrians, made prisoners and carried to Assyria in the time of Hoshea, king of Israel, and in the time of Hezekiah, king of Jerusalem, as can be seen in the fourth book of the Kings, seventeenth chapter, etc."

In his first chapter, which is entirely devoted to this subject, Father Duran quotes several times from the Old Testament, but relies mainly on a citation from the Book of Esdras, where he reads that "they went to live in a land, remote and separated, which had never been inhabited, to which they had a long and tedious journey of a year and a half, for which reason it is supposed these people are found in all the islands and lands of the ocean constituting the Occident."

It is, to say the least, amusing to see the restraint under which men studied and wrote in the sixteenth century. Father Duran brings his arguments to a close by saying that there can be no doubt as to conclusions; "*but in all I submit myself to the correction of the Holy Catholic Church.*" *

Gregorio Garcia, who resided nine years in Peru, in his *Origin of the Indians* (Madrid, 1729), enlarges on Duran's plan and gives numberless supposed similarities between the Mexicans and Hebrews in character, dress, religion, physical peculiarities, condition, customs, and language.

Lord Kingsborough in a most scholarly and dignified way tries to prove the same theory. He also gives an extended list of similarities between the Jews and the Mexicans. Among other things he says: "It is probable that the Toltecs were acquainted with the sin of the first man, committed at the suggestion of the woman, herself deceived by the serpent, who tempted her with the fruit of the forbidden tree, who was the origin of all our calamities, and by whom death came into the world." †

---

* *Historia de las Indias*, vol. i, p. 3.
† Quoted by Bancroft, *Native Races*, vol. v, p. 85.

ORIGIN OF THE MEXICANS. 69

"The character and history of Christ and Huitzilopochtli present certain analogies."*
"The Mexicans applied the blood of sacrifices to the same uses as the Jews."†
For an excellent *résumé* of all the interesting and curious analogies contained in Lord Kingsborough's voluminous work, see Bancroft's *Native Races*, vol. v, pp. 80-91 inclusive. Suffice it here to say that this enthusiastic, almost fanatical advocate of the Jewish discovery of America finds something parallel in Mexican traditions to the entire biblical history from Eden to Calvary.

Mr. James Adair, who lived and traded for forty years with the American Indians (London, 1775), is a warm advocate of this same theory, following in the footsteps of Garcia. Professor Short (p. 143) gives the names of a number of learned authors who practically agree with Duran and Garcia.

Circumstantial evidence has not been lacking in our country toward the support of this theory. In 1815 Mr. James Merrick, of Pittsfield, Mass., found, while plowing, what seemed to be a black strap about six inches in length. On trying to cut it he "found it was formed of two pieces of thick rawhide, sewed and made water-tight with the sinews of some animal, and gummed over; and in the fold

* Kingsborough. † *Idem*.

was contained four folded pieces of parchment." *
One piece was, unfortunately, destroyed, but when the other pieces were taken to Harvard College they were discovered to be quotations in Hebrew from the Old Testament.

More recently, in the State of Ohio, in the heart of a mound was discovered a stone casket, which on being opened was found to contain a slab of stone eight inches long and four and a half inches wide at one end and three at the other, with writing which the Episcopal rector of Newark pronounced to be the Ten Commandments in ancient Hebrew.†

In my library I have an old book published in Mexico in 1807, *Decree of Napoleon, Emperor of the French, on the Jews*, etc. This curious old book, written by Juan Lopez Cancelada, claims that after the captivity the ten tribes of Israel migrated as far as Tartary at first. Then later they passed over the Straits of Anian (Behring) and spread over the American continent. Cancelada appeals to the letters of William Penn to prove (p. 98) that the Quakers found the Indians of Pennsylvania using the Hebrew language, names, coins, and customs.

The same author cites two finds of elephant bones in Mexico—one at Guadalupe Hidalgo, in 1784,

---

* *Native Races*, vol. v, p. 93.   † *Idem.*, p. 94.

ORIGIN OF THE MEXICANS. 71

and the other at Aguascalientes, in 1795—and says that the Jews brought them across the straits on rafts.

Mr. George Jones in his work colonizes this continent with "a remanent of the inhabitants of Tyre who escaped from their island city when it was besieged by Alexander the Great in 332 B. C." *

3. Concerning the colonists from India it is only necessary to say that it rests on analogies between Buddhism and the religion of the early Mexicans, pointed out by Humboldt, Tschudi, Viollet-Leduc, Count Stolberg, and some others. The presence of the serpent among Mexican antiquities is everywhere manifest, and Baron Humboldt thinks he sees "the famous serpent Kaliya or Kaluiaga conquered by Vishnu, . . . and in the Mexican Tonatiuh, the Hindoo Krishna sung of in the Bhagavata-Purana." †

4. The Chinese theory is warmly advocated by our worthy missionary, Rev. Dr. McMaster, of San Francisco, Cal. Perhaps the first writer in modern times to call attention to this theory was the celebrated French Sinologist Deguines, in

---

* *Original History of Ancient America, Founded on the Ruins of Antiquity; The Identity of the Aborigines with the People of Tyrus and Israel, and the Introduction of Christianity by the Apostle St. Thomas* (London, 1843).

† Short, p. 466.

Memoires de l'Academie des Inscriptiones et Belles-Lettres, vol. xxviii (Paris, 1761). He found in the history of Li Yan Tcheon, written in the seventeenth century, the account of a Buddhist missionary who returned in 499 A. D. "from a long journey of discovery to the remote and unknown East." The distance given is about 20,000 Chinese li, or about 6,666 miles. In 1841 Dr. Neuman, of Munich, after mastering the Chinese language, published a translation of this story which may be seen in Charles G. Leland's *Fusang, or the Chinese Discovery of America* (New York, 1875).

These published accounts of what the Hori-Shin saw seem very significant to the traveler in Mexico. There is a considerable resemblance between the Otomí, spoken in Mexico, and the Chinese. Bancroft thinks the strongest proof upon which the Chinese theory rests is the physical resemblance between the inhabitants, and quotes Taylor, in the *Californian Farmer*, as saying: "I have repeatedly seen instances, both of men and women, who in San Francisco could readily be mistaken for Chinese, their almond-shaped eyes, light complexion, and long braided black hair giving them a marked similarity." Linguistic affinities, while they are found in Mexico, especially in the Otomí, are more common in Peru.

ORIGIN OF THE MEXICANS.

5. The Japanese theory is to us still more plausible. Josiah Priest* thinks that Quetzalcoatl, the great culture hero, that "white saintly personage from the East, was a Japanese."

Vallejo, in his *History of California*, says there were Japanese in that part of Mexico at the time of the conquest, and traces of the Japanese language are still found among the coast tribes. It is also a well-known fact that Japanese coming to Mexico can converse with the Indians of the Hausteca, whom they resemble in stature and facial appearance, as readily as can an Italian with a Spaniard. Mr. Brooks, in 1875, published, in the San Francisco *Evening Bulletin*, a detailed account of forty-one particular instances of Japanese wrecks along the Pacific, and says that he has the records of over one hundred such disasters. He also asserts that a majority of the survivors remained permanently on this side of the water. A well-known general in the Mexican army is the son of a Japanese mariner, who early in this century was driven in his junk off the coast of his native land by a storm, which continued to rage till he was finally picked up by a Mexican vessel and landed in Mazatlan, where he lived and died.

The Hon. Toshiro Fugita, Acting Japanese Con-

---
* *American Antiquities*, etc., Albany, 1838.

sul General in Mexico, tells me that geologists of his country believe that formerly there existed a strip of land, or possibly a series of islands, between California and the ancient empire of the sun.

6. We have purposely left the Phœnician theory till the last because of its seeming importance; not that we consider the foregoing as improbable, but especially because this antedates all other Asiatic theories, and its relation to old Testament history makes it of all-absorbing interest.

When Israel's King David died and his son had succeeded to the throne King Hiram of Tyre wrote a letter of condolence to Solomon (1 Kings v)[x]. It is well known that a warm friendship existed between the two kings. Taking advantage of his friendly disposition, the young king of Israel appealed to Hiram for help in building the temple committed to him by his father and also the palace at Lebanon. This affecting piece of biblical history closes thus: "And the king commanded, and they brought great stones, costly stones, and hewed stones, to lay the foundation of the house. And Solomon's builders and Hiram's builders did hew them, and the stone squarers: so they prepared timber and stones to build the house" (verses 17 and 18).

From the same chapter we learn that 138,000 Jews were engaged in the work at Lebanon, and if an

[x] III

equal number of Phœnicians were employed it made a great army of 276,000 men felling cedars, hewing stone, etc., which great number of men was supported by Solomon, who gave to " Hiram twenty thousand measures of wheat for food to his household, and twenty measures of pure oil ; thus gave Solomon to Hiram year by year." This ancient reciprocity treaty lasted for years, to the mutual benefit of both parties interested. After a while Solomon ceded to Hiram the important port of Ezion-Geber, on the Red Sea. Here, some twenty years after the beginning of their pleasant relations, the two kings built a navy, " and Hiram sent in the navy his servants, shipmen that had knowledge of the sea, with the servants of Solomon " (1 Kings ix, 27). We are told that they went to Ophir for gold, that their ships were built large and strong, after the pattern of the ships of Tarshish, and that " once in three years came the navy of Tarshish, bringing gold, and silver, ivory, and apes, and peacocks " (1 Kings x, 22).

Where was this distant Ophir, this "fruitful region?"* Our commentators and encyclopedists agree that " it is difficult to ascertain its situation." The majority say that it was either in Arabia, India, or Africa. But an old Spanish author, Arias

* Gesenius, in McClintock & Strong's *Encyclopædia*.

Montanus (b. 1527, d. 1598), locates it in Peru, and his view, doubtless, accounts for the following passage in Ben Jonson's *Alchemist* (Act ii, Scene i):

> "Come on, sir; now set your foot on shore
> In Novo Orbe. Here's the rich Peru;
> And there within, sir, are the golden mines,
> Great Solomon's Ophir."

Baron Humboldt locates it at Veragua, United States of Colombia; and Fountaine, in his *How the World Was Peopled* (pp. 259, 260), says: "The Phœnician Ophir, or Ofor, which means in their ancient language the *Western Country*, was Mexico and Central America, the land of gold."

Mr. George Jones, devoting a whole volume to the subject, brings the Phœnicians first to Florida and then into the Gulf of Mexico and Yucatan.

A most interesting paper appeared from the pen of Thomas Crawford Johnston in the *Californian* for November and December, 1892, which revives and sustains with great weight this Phœnician theory. Mr. Johnston resided for a year and a half in the islands of the South Pacific. He not only quotes the biblical facts already referred to, but marks out what he believes to have been the route followed by these most ancient and mysterious of navigators. This route, starting at the head of the Red Sea, comes down to the straits of Bab-el-Man-

ORIGIN OF THE MEXICANS. 77

deb, and from that to the coast of India, on to Ceylon, to Java and Sumatra, thence to Malgrave Island and the Caroline Islands, Tonga, Samoa, and Rappa, thence to Easter Island and on to Mexico and Peru. He claims to have found substructions on several of these islands identical with those found under the remnants of Solomon's temple, especially in the size and shape of the enormous stones, weighing, in some cases, over five tons. These substructions he again connects with analogous ruins in Mexico and Peru.

He then quotes Mr. Rawlinson's description of the Phœnicians, and claims " it is impossible for one to spend even a short time in Samoa without realizing how suitable such a description would be if applied to the Samoans, while each day's observation of them, their habits and customs, would only deepen the conviction that the observer was in contact with a people whose social usages must, at some possibly remote period, have been in very close touch with Hebrew institutions."

He found a tradition on every isle visited that referred their origin " to some land lying in the direction of the setting sun." On one island about midocean he found an old tower forty feet high and the ruins of an ancient and evidently once large city. The natives say that it was occupied by " a powerful people called Anut, who had large vessels in which they made long voyages east and west, many moons being required for these voyages."

Coming to Mexico, Mr. Johnston finds evidence of the presence of the Phœnicians "intensified a thousandfold." Architectural remains and forms of religious worship are clearly Phœnician. "The Roman sacrifice and the idol, half man and half brute, are beyond question those of the Phœnician Baal or Moloch." His picture of the Aztec vase with the fringed disk symbol is certainly striking. He then claims that the great Calendar Stone in the National Museum is "the national monument of a seafaring people in the form of a mariner's compass," in the center of which are "seen the faces of Coh, the Mexican Noah, and his wife, the first recorded navigators, and underneath these the Aztec symbol for water." On this point at least he is sustained by Captain Hoff, late United States Consul at Vera Cruz, who on more than one occasion eloquently related his convictions on this subject to the lecturer.

It is further pointed out that the friendly and intimate relations existing between the ancient Phœnicians and the Egyptians, Hebrews, Assyrians, Babylonians, Greeks, and Persians account for the fact "that in their metallurgy these motives are

ORIGIN OF THE MEXICANS. 79

invariably either Egyptian or Assyrian, while their sculptures usually showed a large admixture of Greek." All this seems true in Mexico.

So, after summoning other analogies, Mr. Johnston goes back to Ezion-geber. where Solomon and Hiram built their navy. " These mariners were no rude, uneducated horde, but a class of men who have passed beyond the merely animal tendency of life, and, rising above fog and miasma, live in an atmosphere mainly intellectual—men who dominate their surroundings, and in touching leave an indelible trace of their presence and influence behind them." " The inhabitants of Zidon and Arvad were thy mariners: thy wise men, O Tyrus, that were in thee, were thy pilots " (Ezek. xxvii, 8).

The commercial supremacy of these Phœnician merchants in ancient times is a well-established fact. Their trading posts were everywhere found in the Mediterranean and out on the Atlantic as far north as the " Tin Islands," as England was then called. That their route to Ceylon was a well-beaten one no one will deny. Neither of these routes required the time assigned in sacred writ to the voyages made at the time of Solomon's reign. Architectural remains, traditions, manners and customs, religious beliefs and practices (and here too we see the Phœnician monotheist, in the process of time, developing into the polytheist), the great Calendar or Compass Stone, and the testimony of some English and not a few Mexican authors, justify Mr. Johnston in landing his Phœnican navigators, as does also Ordoñez, on the coasts of Peru and Mexico about 1000 B. C., which date corresponds with the dates given in the Bible narrative of the historic voyages of Hiram and Solomon and the building of the Jewish temple.*

* Here the lecturer exhibited a model of the Aztec Calendar Stone, and a piece of a large vase in which the sacred fire was kept. This has been recently unearthed near Tezcoco.

LECTURE III.

PREHISTORIC MEXICANS.

LECTURE III.

PREHISTORIC MEXICANS.

WE have no pet theory concerning the first inhabitants of Mexico, but believe there is a foundation of truth in several of the theories mentioned in the preceding lecture.

No one can travel along the Pacific coast and throughout the territory of our next-door neighbor without finding everywhere evidence of the presence of Mongolian blood, languages and religions, manners and customs. It seems probable that the wars of the Tartars drove many a colony across the strait or the ocean to this continent.

The Phœnician navigators perhaps antedated these, while from the mysterious Atlantis, so long since submerged beneath the ocean billows, nomadic tribes may have spread themselves far and near over the continent, contemporaneous with, or even prior to, the construction of Solomon's temple. No doubt Clavigero is right in saying that the Americans descended from different nations.

But Gregorio Garcia, who was so narrow-minded that he could see nothing except through Spanish spectacles, and thought all Mexicans sprang from one family, provokes a smile from some of his arguments, especially when he tries to explain away the multiplicity of tongues by saying that "Satan prompted the Indians to learn various languages in order to prevent the extension of the true faith."

This is not so strange when we recall the equally amusing fact that the president of Yale College, Rev. Ezra Stiles, D.D., in 1783, when preaching before the governor of the State of Connecticut appealed to the famous Dighton Rock, in Narragansett Bay, graven, as he believed, in the old Punic or Phœnician character and language, "in proof that the Indians were of the accursed seed of Canaan, and were to be dispelled and rooted out by the European descendants of Japhet."*

Such statements are as smile-provoking as the one so frequently quoted from Mexican mythology by certain materialistic authors who strive to give it the color of authority, and, leaning to the autochthonic theory of the race on this continent, calmly cite their origin as follows: "The races descended from six brothers, sons of the old Ixtacmixcohuatl and of his wife, Ilaneucy."

Ixtacmixcohuatl means a white cloud in the shape of a snake, and refers to the Milky Way (*via*

* *Native Races*, vol. v, 74.

lactea). Ilaneuey means old frog, and *rana*, or frog, is the earth; thus the mother is the old earth. Now one of the sons of the heavens and the earth was Otomitl, the first of the human race.*

Who does not see here, even in this myth, evidence that the first Otomís had, somehow, heard something of the God of heaven stooping down to the garden of Eden and making man out of "the dust of the earth?" But when a recognized Church author solemnly asserts that angels from heaven picked up Asiatics by the hair of the head and, safely conveying them across the Pacific, set them on Mexican *terra firma* to inhabit this continent, and the learned Father Duran, after years of study, reaches the conclusion that a divine revelation is necessary to arrive at the truth of this matter, certainly a novice may well hesitate to be too positive in the advocacy of any single theory.

Besides, whether primitive Mexican races came from Africa or Asia, or from both, the fact remains that they were there, and there ages before Ferdinand ever ruled or Columbus dreamed of seeking new worlds. Indeed, it was quite likely that their coming was contemporaneous with the first footprints of man in Europe, and possibly when their ancient hieroglyphs and picture paintings are fully

* *Mexico á Traves de los Siglos*, vol. i, p. 65.

deciphered we may have a history as old as that of India, China, or Egypt.

Perhaps the most valuable of all recently published histories on Mexico is a monumental work of five large folio volumes entitled *Mexico Á Travès de los Siglos*—Mexico Through the Ages. It is the combined effort of five of the best native writers of present times,* who represent in themselves nearly every school of thought in the country.

This valuable work, in common with most histories of Mexico, opens with the assertion that these races originally inhabited the country lying to our south: the Otomí in central Mexico; the Maya-Quiche, to the south, especially in Yucatan, and migrating tribes in the north generally known as the Nahuas. The existence of these races at a very early period, perhaps three thousand years before the Christian era, as some writers claim, is proven in a variety of ways. The peculiar make of hatchets, knives, and arrowheads, of obsidian, serpentine stone, and silex, and other hard substances found wherever these races flourished is evidence of a very remote period.

Señor Orozco y Barra lays much stress on his linguistic research, and from it not only claims

---

* Juan de Dios Arias, Alfredo Chavero, General Vicente Riva Palacios, José Maria Vigil, Julio Zarate.

great antiquity for the Mayas, but finds fifteen different languages or dialects in Central America and the West India islands related to the Maya language.

The amulets and little idols, also used as ornaments on the person, which are being unearthed in many parts, notably in Tuyahualco and Teotihuacan, both of which cities were doubtless buried ages ago by volcanic eruptions, but are now yielding up their long-hidden treasures, are all of rudimentary state and prove the backwardness of a primitive age. In some parts these amulets and idols represent a later period, and are found of greatly superior workmanship and made of obsidian, of copper, and of gold.* The palaces of Palenque, Mitla, Papantla, and others must have been built in those remote ages. The pyramids of Cholula and Teotihuacan have withstood earthquakes and kept their heads above the vomiting of angry volcanoes for unnumbered cycles. The fossils of mastodons, elephants, oxen, zebras, horses, and other animals frequently found are mute but powerful witnesses to the animal life of the continent in the remote past, while human skeletons of immense size, exhumed chiefly on the Gulf Coast, give rise to the fables, perpetuated during the colonial period, of the ex-

---

*The lecturer exhibited numerous amulets, idols, and obsidian articles unearthed in different localities.

istence of giants contemporaneous with or prior to the times of the Otomís, the Mayas, and the Nahuas. Of these, then, the Maya-Quiches were the most ancient. Tradition, records, and architectural remains all combine to testify that this great family is the oldest on the continent; at least, if not the oldest, the first of which any record can be found. In the fertile valley of the River Usumasinta, south of the Tehuantepec Isthmus, was the cradle of American civilization, " a civilization which was old and ripe when the Toltecs came in contact with it. Under the shadow of the magnificent and mysterious ruins of Palenque a people grew to power who spread into Guatemala and Honduras, northward toward Anahuac and southward into Yucatan, and for a period of probably twenty-five centuries exercised a sway which at one time excited the envy and fear of its neighbors.

"We are fully aware of the uncertainty which attaches itself to tradition in general, and of the caution with which it should be accepted in treating of the foundations of history; but still, with reference to the origin and growth of Old World nations, nothing better offers itself in many instances than suspicious legends. The histories of the Egyptians, the Trojans, the Greeks, and of even ancient Rome rest on no surer footing. It is certain that

PREHISTORIC MEXICANS. 89

while the legendary history of any nation may be confused, exaggerated, and besides full of breaks, still there are some main and fundamental facts out of which it has grown, and this, we think, is especially true of the New World tradition."*

The founder of this great empire was one Votan, who arrived on these western shores about 1000 B. C. Of him Clavigero writes : "They say that Votan, the grandson of that respectable old man who built the great ark to save himself and family from the deluge, and one of those who undertook the building of that lofty edifice which was to reach up to heaven, went by express command of the Lord to people that land." †

To this Professor Short adds: "The tradition of Votan, the founder of the Maya culture, though somewhat warped, probably by having passed through priestly hands, is nevertheless one of the most valuable pieces of information which we have concerning the ancient Americans. Without it our knowledge of the origin of the Mayas would be a hopeless blank, and the ruins of Palenque would be more a mystery than ever. According to this tradition Votan came from the East, from Valum Chivim, by the way of Valum Votan, from across

* Short, p. 204.
† *Hist. ant. de Mexico* (English translation, 1807), vol. 5.

the sea by divine command, to apportion the land of the new continent to seven families which he brought with him."*

His exact starting-point and the means by which he reached the New World cannot be proven. He is said to have made four journeys to his native land, and finally to have mysteriously disappeared. His achievements, while here, were as great as those we read of in connection with any ancient hero. His great city, " Nachan " (city of the serpents), is believed by many to be identical with Palenque. So rapid was the growth of his empire that Votan founded three tributary monarchies. Toward the close of his career he wrote a book in order to record his deeds and prove that he was a "chane," or serpent. This work was scrupulously guarded by the people of Tacoaloya, in Soconusco, for many generations, but finally discovered by the Bishop of Chiapas, Francisco Nuñez de la Vega. It was in the Tzendal language. By the aid of an Indian he managed to read a part of it, and after publishing in his *Constituciones* some general statements about Votan and his having seen the Tower of Babel, like a true son of the Church and a genuine Vandal the old bishop committed the precious document to the flames, in 1691.

* *North Americans of Antiquity*, p. 204.

Other copies, however, seem to have gotten into existence; for Ramon de Ordoñez, of Chiapas, had one as late as the close of the eighteenth century, and, like the one above referred to, had for its title, *Proof That I am a Culebra;* that is, a snake, which title he proves in the body of the work by saying that "he is a Culebra because he is Chivim."

It should be remembered that the symbol of life and power among the Mexicans and Central Americans has always been a serpent. Of this one is constantly reminded in going through the National Museum in the capital.

Pablo Feliz Cabrera, in speaking of the movements of the children of Israel, says in his *Teatro Critico:* "Others had their dwellings about the skirts of Mount Hermon, beyond Jordan to the eastward of Canaan. Of these last were Cadmus and his wife, Hermione or Hermonia, both memorable in sacred as well as profane history, as their exploits occasioned their being exalted to the rank of deities, while in regard to their metamorphosis into snakes (culebras), mentioned by Ovid (*Metam.*, lib. iii), their being Hivites may have given rise to this fabulous transmutation, the name in the Phœnician language implying a snake, which the ancient Hebrew writers suppose to have been given from this people being accustomed to live in caves under ground like snakes."

A little further on in his book Cabrera reaches the conclusion that the Votanites were Carthaginians. This conjecture of his may throw some light upon this strange and wonderfully mysterious people, concerning whom no student of American history can afford to be indifferent. For while, as Professor Short says, "some of the details of the Votanic tradition are not worthy of a moment's consideration, it is quite certain that in the general facts we have a key to the origin of what all Americanists agree in pronouncing the oldest civilization on this continent."

Señor Orozco y Barra seems convinced that this people had their earliest home on the Atlantic coast of the United States, that they passed from Florida into Cuba, and thence into Yucatan, while some, Pimentel among others, find their early home in the valley of our own Mississippi.

We have called them Maya-Quiches. It does not seem quite clear whether a branch of the Maya received the name Quiches, or whether the Quiches amalgamated with the Mayas. Professor Short thinks them a branch of the great Maya family but developing their own institutions, dialects, etc.

Señor Pimentel says that the name Quiche was

applied to the first empire of Palenque, and signified "many trees," and that it was employed by the "innumerable families of different nations which composed it, to symbolize its various branches."

"The tradition of their origin states that they came from the far East, across immense tracts of land and water; that in their former home they had multiplied considerably and lived without civilization and with but few wants; they paid no tribute, spoke a common language, did not bow down to wood and stone, but, lifting their eyes toward heaven, observed the will of their Creator; they attended with respect the rising of the sun, and saluted with their invocations the morning star; with loving and obedient hearts they addressed their prayers to Heaven for the gift of offspring: 'Hail, Creator and Maker! regard us, attend us. Heart of Heaven, Heart of Earth, do not forsake us; do not leave us. God of Heaven and Earth, Heart of Heaven, Heart of Earth, consider our posterity always. Accord us repose, a glorious repose, peace and prosperity, justice, life, and our being. Grant to us, O, Hurakan, to be enlightened and fruitful, thou who comprehendest all things great and small!'"

The National Book of the Quiches is one of the richest mythological legacies left us by primitive people. It is known by the name of *Popol Vuh*, and for what we know of it we are indebted to Dr. C. Scherzer, of Vienna, and Abbé Brasseur de Bourbourg, as well as to a Dominican father named Ximenes, who was curate in the little Indian town of Chichicastenango, among the mountains of Guatemala. This Spanish curate, "noted for his learning and love of the truth," died in the early part of the eighteenth century and left many valuable manuscripts. It is generally supposed that his *exposé* of the ill-treatment of the Indians by the colonial authorities was sufficient cause for their partial destruction and total suppression. Some, however, after remaining hid for long years in an obscure corner of the Dominican convent of Gautemala, came to light on the suppression of all religious orders, and were deposited in the library of the University of San Carlos in that city. In 1854 the traveler and author, Dr. Scherzer, found there this famous *Popol Vuh*, as translated from the Quiche into Spanish by Father Ximenes, and this he carefully copied and published in Vienna in 1856.

Abbé de Bourbourg says that Ximenes discovered it toward the last of the seventeenth century, but, being dissatisfied with Ximenes's translation, he went himself to live among the descendants

PREHISTORIC MEXICANS. 95

of the Maya-Quiches till he "elaborated a new and literal translation."

Bancroft believes the native Quiche to have been so thoroughly under the influence of the Spanish friar that, "consciously or unconsciously, a tinge of biblical expression has influenced the form of the narrative." But he adopts the language and conclusions of Professor Max Müller in saying, "Much remains in these American traditions which is so different from anything else in the national literatures of other countries that we may safely treat it as the genuine growth of the intellectual soil of America." In his third volume on *Native Races* Bancroft gives an excellent condensation of the translation of *Popol Vuh*, referred to by both Bourbourg and Scherzer. Perhaps the most interesting of all is the Quiche account of the creation. "In rude, strange eloquence and poetic originality it is one of the rarest relics of aboriginal thought." The English translation runs as follows:

"And the heaven was formed, and all the signs thereof set in their angle and alignment, and its boundaries fixed toward the four winds by the Creator and Former, and Mother and Father of life and existence—he by whom all move and breathe, the Father and Cherisher of the peace of nations and of the civilization of his people—he whose wisdom has projected the excellence of all that is on the earth, or in the lakes, or in the sea.

"Behold the first word and the first discourse. There was as yet no man, nor any animal, nor bird, nor fish, nor crawfish, nor any pit, nor ravine, nor green herb, nor any tree; nothing was but the firmament. The face of the earth had not yet appeared—only the peaceful sea and all the space of heaven. There was nothing yet joined together, nothing that clung to anything else; nothing that balanced itself, that made the least rustling, that made a sound in the heaven. There was nothing that stood up; nothing but the quiet water, but the sea, calm and alone in its boundaries; nothing existed; nothing but immobility and silence, in the darkness, in the night."

After the creation of the vegetables and lower animal life the narration continues:

"Again the gods took counsel together; they determined to make man. So they made a man of clay, and when they had made him they saw that it was not good. He was without cohesion, without consistence, motionless, strengthless, inept, watery; he could not move his head, his face looked but one way; his sight was restricted, he could not look behind him; he had been endowed with language, but he had no intelligence, so he was consumed in the water.

"Again is there counsel in heaven: 'let us make an intelligent being who shall adore and invoke us.' It was decided that a man should be made of wood and a woman of a kind of pith. They were made; but the result was in no way satisfactory. They moved about perfectly well, it is true; they increased and multiplied; they peopled the world with sons and daughters, little wooden manikins like themselves; but still the heart and the intelligence were wanting; they held no memory of their Maker and Former; they lived a useless existence; they lived as the beasts live; they forgot the Heart of Heaven. They were but an essay, an attempt at men; they had neither blood, nor substance, nor moisture, nor fat; their cheeks were shriveled, their feet and hands dried up; their flesh languished.

"Then was the Heart of Heaven wroth, and he sent ruin and destruction upon those ingrates; he rained upon them night and day from heaven with a thick resin, and the earth was darkened. And the men went mad with terror; they tried to mount upon the roofs, and the houses fell; they tried to climb the trees, and the trees shook them far from their branches; they tried to hide in the caves and the dens of the earth, but these closed their holes against them. The bird Xecotcovach came to tear out their eyes, and the Camalotz cut off their head, and the Cotzbalam devoured their flesh, and the Tecumbalam broke and bruised their bones to powder. Thus were they all devoted to chastisement and destruction, save only a few who were preserved as memorials of the wooden men that had been; and these now exist in the woods as little apes.

"Once more are the gods in council; in the darkness, in the night of a desolated universe, do they commune together; 'Of what shall we make man?' And the Creator and Former made four perfect men, and wholly of yellow and white maize (corn) was their flesh composed. These were the names of the four men that were made: the name of the first was Balam-Quitze; of the second, Balam-Agab; of the third, Mahucutah; and of the fourth, Iqi-Balam. They had neither father nor mother, neither were they made by the ordinary agents in the work of creation; but their coming into existence was a miracle extraordinary, wrought by the special intervention of Him who is preeminently the Creator. Verily, at last, were there found men worthy of their origin and their destiny; verily, at last, did the gods look on beings who could see with their eyes, and handle with their hands, and understand with their hearts. Grand of countenance and broad of limb, the four sires of our race stood up under the white rays of the morning star—sole light as yet of the primeval world—stood up and looked. Their great clear eyes swept rapidly over all; they saw the woods and the rocks, the lakes and the sea, the mountains and the valleys, and the heavens that were above all; and they comprehended all and admired exceedingly. Then they returned thanks to those who had made the world and all that therein was: 'We offer up our thanks, twice—yea, verily, thrice. We have received life; we speak, we walk, we taste; we hear and understand; we know both that which is near and that which is far off; we see all things, great and small, and in all the heaven and earth. Thanks, then, Maker and Former, Father and Mother of our life! We have been created; we are.'

" But the gods were not wholly pleased with this thing; heaven, they thought, had overshot its mark; these men were too perfect; knew, understood, and saw too much. Therefore there was counsel again in heaven: 'What shall we do with man now? It is not good, this that we see; these are as gods; they would make themselves equal with us; lo, they know all things, great and small. Let us now contract their sight, so that they may see only a little of the surface of the earth and be content.' Thereupon the Heart of Heaven breathed a cloud over the pupil of the eyes of men, and a veil came over it as when one breathes on the face of a mirror. Thus was the globe of the eye darkened; neither was that which was far off clear to it any more, but only that which was near.

"Then the four men slept, and there was counsel in heaven; and four women were made. To Balam-Quitze was allotted Caha-Paluma to wife; to Balam-Agab, Chomiha; to Mahucutah, Tzununiha; and to Iqi-Balam, Cakixaha. Now the women were exceedingly fair to look upon; and when the men awoke their hearts were glad because of the women.

"They had as yet no worship save the breathing of the instinct of their soul, as yet no altars to the gods; only—and is there not a whole idyl in the simple words?—only they gazed up into heaven, not knowing what they had come so far to do! They were filled with love, with obedience, and with fear; and lifting their eyes toward heaven they made their requests"—in the following language, part of which might have been used by King David himself:

"Hail! O Creator, O Former! thou that hearest and understandest us! abandon us not, forsake us not! O God, thou that art in heaven and on the earth, O Heart of Heaven, O Heart of Earth! give us descendants and a posterity as long as the light endure. Give us to walk always in an open road, in a path without snares; to lead happy, quiet, and peaceable lives, free of all reproach." It was thus they spake, living tranquilly, invoking the return of the light, waiting the rising of the sun, watching the star of the morning, precursor of the sun.

The account of their migrations which follows is so confused as to make it improbable that the locations named should be fully identified. But it is clear that in their original home they became weary of watching for the rising sun, that is, the coming of temporal power. Then it was the four men started on their journey to Tulanzuiva, the seven caves or ravines. On their arrival a different deity was assigned to each. Henceforward their worship is more material and ceremonial.

Tulan was found to have a colder climate than their eastern home, and the god Tohil created artificial heat. "But incessant rains, accompanied with hail, extinguished all their fires, which were again rekindled repeatedly by the fire god." But Tulan, with its rains, extreme cold, dampness, and famines, followed by the confusion of tongues, proved an unfavorable locality for their permanent abode. So at last this mysterious land of the seven caves, this Tulan, was abandoned, and under the leadership of Tohil they migrated through dense forests, over high mountains, through a long sea, which parted at their coming, and by a rough and pebbly shore, till at last, their tribulations ended, they reached the beautiful Hacavitz—a mountain named after their god.

"Here they were informed that the sun would appear, and as a consequence the four progenitors of the race and all the people rejoiced. Here was everything beauteous and gladdening. The morning star shed forth a resplendent brightness, and the sun itself at last appeared, though then it had not the warmth which it possessed at a later day. Before the light of the sun, however, the gods of Tohil, Avilix, and Hacavitz, together with the tigers and lions and reptiles, were changed into stone."

To interpret this paragraph, which is greatly condensed, is a difficult undertaking; still, there are certain facts which seem to serve as the basis of intelligent speculation. The language is extremely figurative throughout the narrative, and especially so here. Their worship of the morning star at an early period seems to connect them with the Mediterranean people of the Old World. The allusions to the sun not yet having come may be retrospective, indicating that the worship of the sun had not been adopted at that early date, or it may indicate that the period of national strength had not dawned.

The fact that the morning star shone more brilliantly on Mount Hacavitz than at Tulan (the seven caves) may mean either that the worship of the star was more specially celebrated, or it may have reference to an astronomical fact, that the star itself was more luminous, and furnish evidence in harmony with the statements of the narrative that Mount Hacavitz was a more southern location than the tempestuous Tulan.

The petrifaction of the three tribal gods may have been the result of an age of peace and prosperity which offered an opportunity for developing their cultus; or, upon the other hand, if the coming of the sun refers to the advent of a new religion, that which is known to have prevailed among the Nahuas, the old gods may have been sculptured in stone, that their national character and deeds might not be forgotten before the increasing importance of the new faith. There they instituted sacrifices of beasts to the three stone gods Tohil, Avilix, and Hacavitz; they even drew blood from their own bodies and offered it to them.

" Finally, not content with these, the first four men, led by Balam-Quitze, instituted human sacrifices. Captives were taken from native tribes, kidnapping was practiced extensively, until the hostility of their neighbors broke forth into open war. The contest, however, resulted favorably to the Quiches, and the surrounding tribes became subject to the victorious power. In Hacavitz they composed a national song called the Kamucu (We see), a memorial of their misfortunes in Tulan—a lament for the loss of so many of their people in that unfortunate locality. This loss is described as occasioned by a portion of their race being left behind, rather than as the result of the misfortunes which attended them there. At last, at the noonday of their national glory, it came to pass that the ancestors of their race, Balam-Quitze, died—the men who came from the East, from across the sea, died—and their remains were enveloped in a great bundle and preserved as memorials of the ancestors of the race. Then the Quiches sang the sad Kamucu, and mourned the loss of their leaders and that portion of their race which they left behind them in Tulan."

The exact location of Tulan is a subject of dispute among historians. Four different places with this same name are certainly mentioned in *Popol Vuh*, two across the sea and two on this continent. Orozco y Barra is doubtless right in locating one at about fifty miles north of the present capital of Mexico, and which place in these times is called Tula, a place, by the way, where fire is still needed, and which corresponds in other respects to the description of Tolan in the ancient National Book.

The other and later Tolan was doubtless in the State of Chiapas, near the ancient city of Xibalba. In the Tolan north of Anahuac (what is now Mexico's national capital) the Maya-Quiches doubtless mingled with the Nahuas, and after appropriating certain elements of their language, worship, and other customs, migrated southward again and established the Quiche-Cakchiquel monarchy in Guatemala about the eleventh century. Colonies spread further south into various parts of Central America, where remnants of their people and evidences of their former glory are found to this day.

The purely Maya branch of the family are found in considerable numbers in the State of Yucatan, and are the admiration of all travelers, their cleanliness, their intelligence and quiet habits being marked characteristics of the race. Yet in time of war they are remarkably brave and heroic. This last characteristic certainly gives color to the claim made by some writers concerning what they are pleased to call an heroic period in the history of the Mayas, a period which occupies the same place in their history as the Trojan war does in the history of Greece. "The tradition of the fall of Xibalba, the terror of its neighbors, the power which by its enemies was called infernal, is an heroic composition founded on a combination of events as mysterious and wonderful as those contained in the 'Iliad' itself. To locate the events in their proper place, to assign them their true period, is attended with as many difficulties as attend the Homeric history."

We have given more space to this Maya race than we intend to give to any other, and for various reasons. First, it is the earliest race with anything like a record on the continent, and we believe that all Americanists will give more attention to this cradle of American civilization in the future than they have in the past.

Max Müller well says, "The Usumacintas seem a kind of central point for the high culture of Central America;"* and the famous explorer Charnay adds, "Palenque will probably some day decide the question of American civilization. It only awaits a Champollion."

We, the possessors of a higher and purer civilization—of a Christian civilization—cannot afford to be entirely indifferent to their past, especially since we are trying to lead the descendants of this noble though oppressed race "from darkness to light." For all the promising work now carried on by the evangelical Churches south of the Rio Grande

* *Amerikanische Urreligionen*, p. 456.

PREHISTORIC MEXICANS. 107

none is so full of hope as work among these and other indigenous races.

We now come to another chapter of legendary history which is difficult to treat, difficult because so misty. We refer to the races occupying the central and northern part of the country in pre-Toltec times. These are generally known as the Nahua nations, and divided into at least eight families. Bancroft arranges them as follows: Quinames, Olmecs, Xicalancas, Totonacs, Huastecs, Miztecs, Zapotecs, and Otomís. Señor Orozco y Barra says that the Cuicatecs, Triquis, Chiniantecs, Mazatecs, Chatinos, Papabucos, Soltecos, Chontales, and Cohuicas belong to the same times. Prichard, in his *Natural History of Man* (vol. ii, p. 512), adds the Coras, Tepanecs, and Tarascos. The Codices Vaticanus and Tellerianus give the names as follows: Olmecs, Xicalancas, Chichimecs, Nonohualcas, Michinacas, Conixcas, Totonacs, and Cuextecas.

In the light of the most recent investigation none of these lists is entirely satisfactory. Doubtless different names have been given to the same tribe, and in some cases the names simply refer to families of one and the same nation. We cannot pretend to "be wise above another" in the matter, and can only follow our humble judgment in a case which seems to us to require more light from honest and learned investigators before one can speak with any degree of certainty.

The chief authority for this uncertain history is the Codex Chimalpopoca. It is an anonymous record written in Aztec, but with Spanish letters, copied by Ixtlilxochitl, and belonged to the famous Boturini collection. Even this has never been published, and is only known by occasional references to it contained in the works of Brasseur de Bourbourg. From the abbé we quote the following:

"This is the beginning of the history of things which came to pass long ago, of the division of the earth, the property of all, the origin and its foundation, as well as the manner in which the sun divided it six times four hundred plus one hundred plus thirteen years ago to-day, the twenty-second of May, 1558;"* that is, 955 B.C., a date accepted by most Spanish and Mexican authors, and, strangely enough, it corresponds exactly with the date admitted by Dr. J. W. Foster in his *Prehistoric Races*. †

In the list of pre-Toltec nations above mentioned the Quinames come first, and are generally called giants, the name signifying men of great stature. They are traditionally assigned as the first inhabitants of nearly every part of the country. Torquemada and Veytia reject the idea that a race of giants

---

* Bancroft's *Natives Race*, vol. v, p. 193. † P. 342.

actually existed, but Duran gives it as a fact. Clavigero says: "Nor can we be persuaded that there has ever been, as those writers imagined, a whole nation of giants, but only single individuals."* In the National Museum of Mexico may be seen a skeleton found on the gulf coast, and said to be that of Negro Quiname, which stands over seven feet high. Several other facts are quoted as evidence that these giants were probably Negroes. Among the great variety of idols frequently discovered in excavations now going on at Teotihuacan many are found representing African features, the large nose and thick lips being especially noticeable. In 1860, in the Hacienda de Hueyapan, State of Vera Cruz, workmen accidentally unearthed a gigantic head of granite nearly five feet high and of corresponding proportions. The features are clearly Ethiopian. Later a great stone hatchet was found with a face carved on the handle also containing Ethiopian features. It is easy to believe that both of these may have been buried three thousand years. The Negroes may have been one or separate races, or perhaps, as Chavero says, the former were like "a passing bird" pushed on to the coast by the superior numbers of the latter or, possibly, in quest of a warmer climate.

*Vol. i, p. 111.

Oviedo and Mendoza say that the giants came from the Strait of Magellan, and Boturini could give no reason for doubting their existence.* "Being large in stature, they could out-travel the rest of mankind, and thus became naturally the first settlers of distant parts of the world." They were destroyed in the first or second century of our era. Whether giants or not, they were a barbarous race, living like brutes of the field, "addicted to the most disgusting vices," especially drunkenness to excess. Ixtlilxochitl says that they were exterminated by a great convulsion of nature; but Father Duran says that all the males were destroyed by the Tlascaltecas during a great banquet prepared for the purpose in 107 A. D. As some regard the Olmecs an offshoot of the Mayas it may be that "we have here a figurative allusion, from a Nahua standpoint, to the fall of the Xibalban power itself—the New World Babylon, which, like the old, may have met its fate during a drunken revel."

About the time that the Quinames were destroyed the Pyramid of Cholula was built, under the direction of a chief called Xelhua. Its origin is said to have been connected in some way with a flood, but authorities are not agreed as to whether it was built as a memorial in honor of the builders' salva-

* *Native Races*, vol. v, p. 199.

tion from a former flood, or as a place of refuge from another that might come. Boturini and most Spanish writers connect it with the Tower of Babel, claiming that the ancestors of the Olmecs were present on the occasion, and they also say that work on the Cholula tower was stopped by fire sent from heaven. It is true that the Toltecs had a deluge tradition of a general and devastating flood, possibly the scriptural one.

Lord Kingsborough seems to imply that Xelhua was one of those who escaped with Noah in the ark, and from the plain of Shinar led a colony to the New World. This would certainly put the building of Cholula much earlier than is generally claimed, or make Xelhua about one thousand years old when he began the construction of the Mexican tower.

Father Duran, however, gives a different and to us more reasonable cause for the building of the Cholula pyramid, for we have never been able to see why the natives would build a tower to escape a possible flood on the very foothills of " snow capped mountains which kiss the firmament." Father Duran, who wrote soon after the Spanish Conquest, says that he found at Cholula a native one hundred years old, " bent with age," but well informed as to its history. From him Duran took down the following story:

"In the beginning, before the light of the sun had been created, this land was in obscurity and darkness and void of any created thing; all was a plain without hill or elevation, encircled in every part by water, without tree or created thing; and immediately after the light and the sun arose in the east there appeared gigantic men of deformed stature and possessed the land, who, desiring to see the nativity of the sun as well as his occident, proposed to go and seek them. Dividing themselves into two parties, some journeyed toward the west and others toward the east; these traveled until the sea cut off their road, whereupon they determined to return to the place from which they started, and arriving at this place, which was called Iztacculin, ineminian (Cholula), not finding the means of reaching the sun, enamored of his light and beauty, they determined to build a tower so high that its summit should reach the sky. Having collected material for the purpose, they found a very adhesive clay and bitumen, with which they speedily commenced to build the tower, and having reared it to the greatest possible altitude, so that they say it reached to the sky, the Lord of the heavens, enraged, said to the inhabitants of the sky, 'Have you observed how they of the earth have built a high and haughty tower to mount hither, being enamored of the light of the sun and his beauty? Come and confound them; because it is not right that they of the earth, living in the flesh, should mingle with us.' Immediately, at that very instant, the inhabitants of the sky sallied forth like flashes of lightning; they destroyed the edifice and divided and scattered its builders to all parts of the earth."*

Here, then, in this most ancient of records we find no reference whatever to a flood, but rather a confirmation of the supposed tendency of Americans all over the continent, including those of the Mississippi valley, perhaps, to erect mounds and truncated pyramids for the purpose of worshiping the sun. That these mounds were regarded as sacred is further proven by the fact that recently in the construction of a railway across the corner of the pyramid under consideration the workmen found an ancient sepulcher, and took out two petrified human skeletons. Similar proofs have been discovered at Teotihuacan.

After the Quinames came the Olmecs and the Xicalancas, named after their first rulers, Olmecatl and Xicalancatl. These are sometimes represented as two nations, but both using the Toltec language, though settled in Anahuac long before the estab-

* Duran, vol. i, p. 6.

lishment of the Toltec empire in Tula. While as nations they lost their identity before the coming of Cortez, yet under new names and other family combinations they were still living in Puebla, southern Vera Cruz, Chiapas, and Tabasco at the time of the conquest. They are generally considered as the first of the Nahua nations in central Mexico, and tradition on the Campeche coast says that they came there in ships from the east, and afterward migrated both north and south. A cape in the State of Campeche still bears the name of Xicolanco. They were an industrious and quiet people, being especially devoted to agriculture.

It is also claimed that the Olmecs built the famous Palenque, the oldest city on the American continent,* but now one of the grandest of Mexican ruins. Of it the modern poet has written:

> "Unlike Copan, yet buried, too, 'mid trees
> Upspringing there for sumless centuries,
> Behold a royal city, vast and lone,
> Lost to each race, to all the world unknown,
> Like famed Pompeii, 'neath her lava bed,
> Till chance unveiled the City of the Dead.
> Palenque! seat of kings! as o'er the plain,
> Clothed with thick copse, the traveler toils with pain,
> Climbs the rude mound the shadowy scene to trace,
> He views in mute surprise thy desert grace.
> At every step some palace meets his eye,
> Some figure frowns, some temple courts the sky.

* *Native Races*, vol. v, p. 202.

> It seems as if that hour the verdurous earth,
> By genii struck, had given their fabrics birth,
> Save that old Time hath flung his darkening pall
> On each tree-shaded tower and pictured wall."

This ruined city, with all its beautiful and mysterious surroundings, was unknown to the outside world till 1750. In 1787 the ancient ruins were explored by order of the King of Spain, and again in 1807 by a like order. Since then several other European and a few American travelers have visited and described this enchanting spot; and the valuable works of Galindo, Dupaix, Waldeck, Stephens, Charnay, Squire, and Ober furnish as interesting reading as the student of history could desire.

From all these we learn that where once existed the metropolis of a mighty empire in the beautiful valley of Usumacinta, only ruins now exist, ruins which have given rise to almost as many theories as there have been investigators. All, however, seem to unite in this conviction, that this region was the capital of an ancient theocratic empire of vast influence.

On the moss-covered walls of the ruins are sculptures which fain would " speak to us in an unknown language, hieroglyphics, and the chiseled types of a people long since departed." In what is known in modern times as " Casa Number Two " is a portion of a famous sculpture known as the " Palenque Tablet," containing the figure of a cross about which archæolgists have wrangled, and bitterly. In 1842 a portion of it was sent to the National Museum at Washington. A third part is supposed to be buried somewhere about the ruins. Notwithstanding these unfavorable circumstances Professor Charles Rau, of the Smithsonian Institution, through most diligent labor, has produced a restoration of the sculpture as it probably appeared in the "Sanctuary of the Cross" in Palenque. Mr. Stephens has thus described it:

"The principal subject of this tablet is the cross. It is surmounted by a strange bird and loaded with indescribable ornaments. The two figures are evidently those of important personages. They are well drawn, and in symmetry of proportion are perhaps equal to many that are carved on the walls of the temples of Egypt. . . . Both are looking toward the cross, and one seems in the act of making an offering, perhaps of a child. All speculations on the subject are, of course, entitled to a little regard; but perhaps it would not be wrong to ascribe to these personages a sacerdotal character. The hieroglyphics, doubtless, explain all. Near them are other hieroglyphics, which remind us of the Egyptian mode for recording the name, history, office, or character of the persons represented. This tablet of the cross has given rise to more learned speculation than perhaps any others found at Palenque."

How or when the first symbol of the cross was introduced into America is an interesting though perhaps unsatisfactory study. That part, at least, is interesting which claims that one of the twelve apostles brought it here, and fourteen or fifteen centuries before Cortez built his first Christian church in Tlaxcala this same apostle preached the Gospel to the descendants of the Olmecs on the very ground where these ruins are now found.

The hero of General Lew Wallace's *Fair God* in Nahua history goes by the name of Quetzalcoatl. Among the Quiches his name was Gucumatz, and among the Mayas, Cukulcan, which, singularly enough, means the same in each language, namely, "plumed serpent." The first named was no tribal hero, but belonged to the entire Nahua race, and some believe that he was called "feathered or plumed serpent," after the brazen serpent which Moses lifted up in the wilderness. "Representations of the lifting up of serpents frequently occur in Mexican paintings."* Not only so, but the plagues which Moses called down upon the Egyptians by lifting up his rod, which became a serpent, are referred to in some of the pictures found in the Bor-

* *Native Races*, vol. v, p. 87.

gian manuscripts. The name Quetzalcoatl seems to have been applied to the leader or culture hero of the people during hundreds of years of Nahua. At least two different personages bore that name.

About the time that the Olmecs were in the height of their power a man named Quetzalcoatl appeared in the country, "a venerable, just, and holy man, who taught by precept and example the paths of virtue in all the Nahua cities."

Garcia, Torquemada, Sahagun, and other Spanish writers firmly believed him to be identical with St. Thomas, one of the apostles, and repeatedly mentioned him as the first man to preach the Gospel in all America. We cannot see why this tradition is any less groundless than the one which takes St. Thomas to East India, as published in our own cyclopedias.* Of this Carlos de Siguenza and Luis Becerra Tanco, in *Felicidad de Mexico* (p. 55), say that the hero's proper name, Topiltzni Quetzalcoatl, "closely resembles in sound and signification that of Thomas, surnamed Didymus; for *To*, in the Mexican name, is an abbreviation of Tomas, to which *Pilcin*, meaning son or disciple, is added; while the meaning of Quetzalcoatl is exactly the same as that of the Greek name Didymus, a twin, being compounded of *Quetzalli*, a plume of

* See McClintock & Strong, vol. x, p. 368.

green feathers, metaphorically signifying anything precious, and *coatl*, a serpent, metaphorically meaning one of two twins."

Boturini says that he had "certain historical memoranda by the glorious apostle St. Thomas." He also cites paintings of crosses found by him in southern Mexico and other evidences of the "tracks of his holy feet in many parts of New Spain." Of this man or another bearing the same name we shall have more to say in our next lecture. After Quetzalcoatl's mysterious disappearance nothing more is known of Olmec and Xicalanca history till the establishment of the Toltec empire, when they are still in possession of Puebla and Tlaxcala.

The Totonacs were also pre-Toltec in history. They migrated from the valley of Mexico and claim to have built the pyramids of Teotihuacan, a great religious center in primitive times, of which we will speak later.

The Otomís, another primitive race, differ in language from all Nahua nations, though with a slight affinity with the Totonacs, "and have always been to a certain extent an outcast and oppressed race, 'the Jews of Anahuac,' trodden down in succession by Toltec, Chichimec, and Aztec." When the Toltec empire was established they possessed much territory of Anahuac.

Of the early history of the Miztecs, Zapotecs, Huastecs, and other pre-Toltec nations but little is known which would be of interest here. This brings us to the consideration of the more regular and less mythical annals of one of the most enchanting histories in the whole world, and all upon our own continent.

LECTURE IV.

EARLY MEXICANS AND THEIR HISTORY.

LECTURE IV.

THE EARLY MEXICANS AND THEIR HISTORY.

"ONE hundred and sixteen years after wise Toltecs, astrologers, and those of other arts had assembled in Huehue Tlapallan for the purpose of regulating their calendar, the sun and moon were eclipsed, the earth shook and the rocks were rent asunder, and many other things and signs happened, though there was no loss of life. This was the year Ce Calli, which, the chronology being reduced to our systems, proves to be the same date when Christ our Lord suffered." Thus does Ixtlilxochitl, Mexico's best primitive historian, introduce us to the Toltecs.

It will be of interest first to locate the meeting place of this famous convocation, which occurred about 2000 B. C., after one hundred and four years of wandering over land and sea, during which time the ancient Mexicans suffered great hardships.

The etymology of the word Huehue Tlapallan is "ancient red land or land of color." "Astrology, soothsaying, the interpretation of dreams and of auguries, such as the flight or song of birds, the sudden meeting of wild animals, or the occurrence of other unlooked-for events, were regarded by the Nahuas as of the greatest importance, and the practice of such arts was intrusted to the *tonalpouhqui*, 'those who count by the sun,' a class of men held in high esteem, to whom was attributed a perfect knowledge of future events. We have seen that no undertaking, public or private, of any importance could be engaged in except under a suitable and propitious sign, and to determine this sign the *tonalpouhqui* was appealed to. The science of astrology was written down in books kept with great secrecy and mystery, altogether unintelligible to the common crowd, whose good or bad fortune was therein supposed to be painted. The details of the methods employed in the mysterious rites of divination are nowhere recorded."*

Most historians agree that these ancestors of the Toltecs came from the distant East in seven barks or ships, which Sahagun calls Chicomoztoc, or the seven grottoes. In all ages the number seven has been a sacred number among American peoples. It may be well, before passing, to remark that perchance these seven ships, or grottoes, are "the seven caves" so often referred to in primitive Mexican history. The starting point was doubtless

* *Native Races*, vol. ii, p. 500.

some part of Asia and, perhaps, "a plain in the land of Shinar" (Gen. xi, 2). The resting place, which they called Huehue Tlapallan, and which they "found fertile and desirable to dwell in," according to Professor Short, was in the valley of the Mississippi. Mr. Bancroft advocates a southern locality, possibly Honduras. Sahagun thinks it was Florida. Humboldt cites the River Giles in New Mexico, while others place it somewhere on the coast of the Californian Gulf, but, with very few exceptions, Spanish and Mexican historians, including Clavigero and Veytia, unite in locating it north of Anahuac.

On coming from the land where the sun rises to their new home, "which they found to be fertile and desirable to dwell in, . . . the supreme command was in the hand of a chieftain whom history calls Quetzalcohuatli, that is to say, lord *par excellence*. To his care was confided the holy envelope which concealed the divinity from the human gaze, and he alone received from it the necessary instructions to guide his people's march. These kinds of divinities, thus enveloped, passed for being sure talismans, and were looked upon with the greatest respect and veneration. They consisted generally of a bit of wood, in which was inserted a little idol of green stone; this was covered with the skin of a serpent or of a tiger, after which it was rolled in numerous little bands of stuff, wherein it would remain wrapped for centuries together. Such is, perhaps, the origin of the medicine bags made use of even in the present day by the Indians of the Great Desert." *

It is not unlikely that the Nahuas, on first reaching our northwest coast, were few in number, and that they remained there for generations till they became a nation of no mean proportions. After crossing the watershed between the sources of the Columbia and Missouri rivers part wended their way to the Mississippi valley, where their empire continued to spread with the passing ages; while another part made their way into Utah, where we may to-day see their remains in the cliff dwellings of the San Juan valley and the many ruins of Aztec springs.†

The first Nahuas to reach Mexico probably came by ships from the direction of Florida, landed at the mouth of the beautiful broad Panuco (Mexico's Mississippi), and migrated southward till they came into touch with the older and riper civilization of the Mayas. The Toltecs probably came by land, and from the distant north. The Chichimecs, their old neighbors in Huehue Tlapallan, followed them

* *Native Races*, vol. iii, p. 270.
† *North Americans of Antiquity*, p. 517.

and adopted their language. The Nahuatlacas arrived centuries later, and finally the Aztecs reached Anahuac some four hundred years before the Spanish conquest.

Having treated the Maya question in our former lecture, we will take up the others in chronological order.

This leads us first to mention the Toltecs. After long centuries of peace and prosperity in "the red land," Chalcatzin and Tlacamilitzin, chiefs in the royal line, rebelled against the legitimate successor to the throne. After a war of eight years, with their numerous families and allies they were driven out of the country. They settled in Tlapallancoco, the little, or New Tlapallan. Among those who joined the fortunes of the insurgents were five other chiefs, with their respective tribes. Their departure, according to Chavero, took place in the year 583 A. D., though Clavigero claims it was in 544. After remaining three years in Tlapallancoco the seven chiefs held a council to determine whether they should make that their permanent capital or should move further on.* "Then arose a great astrologer named Hueman, or Huematzin, saying that according to their histories they had suffered great persecutions from heaven, but that these had always been

* *Native Races*, vol. v, p. 211.

followed by great prosperity; that their persecutions had always occurred in the year Ce Tecpatl; but that year once passed great blessings ensued; that their trouble was a great evil immediately preceding the dawn of a greater good, and consequently it did not behoove them to remain so near their enemies. Moreover, his astrology had taught him that toward the rising sun there was a broad and happy land, where the Quinames had lived for many years; but so long a time had now passed since their destruction that the country was depopulated; besides, the fierce Chichimecs, their neighbors, rarely penetrated those regions. . . . These and other things did Hueman counsel, and they seemed good to the seven chiefs; so that after three years were passed, or eleven years from the time when they left Huehue Tlapallan, they started on their migration."

After twelve days they reached Hueyxalan, seventy leagues, and remained there for four years. Pushing on they traveled one hundred leagues more and came to Jalisco, the heart of the country. In this place they remained eight years. Subsequently they made eleven other marches, covering, in all, one thousand two hundred and twenty-four leagues, made in one hundred and seventy-eight days. But as they tarried from five to twenty-six years in each place they finally reached Tollan, or Tula, one hundred and nineteen years after leaving their original habitat. This last-named place, about thirty miles to the north of the modern capital of the country, became the center of the wonderful Toltec empire, an empire which had great influence on subsequent Mexican history.

Their government during the journey was theocratic and their religion theistic. They had military chiefs, but God was their great commander, and they relied on Hueman, their chief priest, to know God's will.

Mexican historians find here an interesting parallel with the experiences of the Hebrews, who also made comparatively short marches, were always influenced by religious considerations, and were ever subject to sacerdotal command. One of their most noted living writers says that " the Israelites would never have reached the land of promise if Moses had been a warrior and not a hierarch." The unwritten history of Toltec migrations would doubtless disclose many a triumph of diplomacy as well as of armed aggression.

The exact date of the founding of the Toltec empire in Tollan (Tula), as well as the names of its first kings, have been matters of lively discussion among European and American authors. Most of these, so frequently quoted during these lectures, have imitated the ancient Mexican historian Ixtlilxochitl. Late research, no doubt, gives more accurate information. The *Anales de Cuauhtitlan*, though originally published in the Mexican language between the years of 1563 and 1570, and preserved for long years in the Jesuit College of San Gregorio, were recently translated by Faustino Galicia Chimalpopoca and corrected by Messrs. Ramirez, Mendoza, and Sanchez Solis, all eminent Indian scholars who were within late years connected with the National Museum of Mexico. The result of the united study of these most distinguished archæologists is that Tula was first occupied by the Toltecs in the year Ce Tochtli, that is, the year 674 of the Christian era. For twenty-six years they were under the command of their rebel princes Chalcaltzin and Tlacamihtzin. Then their first king, Mixcoamazatzin, was chosen. He reigned from 700 to 765, and, after him, ten other monarchs, down to the second Quetzalcoatl, who reigned from 1048 to 1116, when the empire was overthrown and Tula destroyed. This covers a period of four hundred and forty-two years.

It seems that the great high priest or astrologer, Hueman, either lived about three hundred years or had successors who carried his name and profession through three centuries, for we find that during the reign of Ixtlilcuechahuac, second king of the empire, "the aged Hueman assembled" all the wise men to join him in his final work on earth.* "At this assembly there were brought forward all the Toltec records, reaching back to the earliest period of their existence, and from these documents, after a long conference and the most careful study, the *Teoamoxtli*, or 'book of God,' was prepared, that is, painted. In its pages were inscribed the Nahua annals from the time of the deluge, or even from the creation, together with all their religious rites, governmental system, laws, and social customs; their knowledge respecting agriculture and all the arts and sciences, particular attention being given to astrology, and a complete explanation of their modes of reckoning time and interpreting the hieroglyphics. To the divine book was added a chapter of prophecies respecting future events and the signs by which it should be known when the time of their fulfillment was drawing near."

Let us here quote the testimony of Clavigero : †

"The Toltecs were the most celebrated people of Anahuac for their superior civilization and skill in arts, whence, in after ages, it has been common to distinguish the most remarkable artists in an hon-

---
* *Native Races*, vol. v, p. 251, and Clavigero, vol. i, p. 115.
† Clavigero, vol. i, p. 114. Richmond edition.

orable manner by the application of Toltecas. They always lived in society collected into cities, under the government of kings and regular laws.

"They were not very warlike, and less turned to the exercise of arms than to the cultivation of the arts. The nations that have succeeded them have acknowledged themselves indebted to the Toltecs for their knowledge of the culture of grain, cotton, pepper, and other most useful fruits. Nor did they only practice those arts which are dictated by necessity, but those also which minister to luxury. They had the art of casing gold and silver and melting them in whatever forms they pleased, and acquired the greatest reputation from the cutting of all kinds of gems; but nothing to us raises their character so high as their having been the inventors, or at least the reformers, of that system of the arrangement of time which was adopted by all the civilized nations of Anahuac, and which, as we shall see afterward, implies numerous observations and a wonderfully correct astronomy."

This is a matter that certainly deserves more than passing mention, and which proves beyond a doubt the high state of civilization reached by these people. In their picture *Teoamoxtli*, or divine book, were described the heavens, the planets, the constellations, the Toltecan calendar, with its cycles,

EARLY MEXICANS AND THEIR HISTORY. 133

etc. Clavigero adds: "However incredible it may appear to the critics of Europe, who are accustomed to look upon the Americans as all equally barbarous, they, Mexicans and all the other civilized nations of Anahuac, regulated their civil year according to the solar."* It "consisted of seventy-three periods of thirteen days, and the century of seventy-three periods of thirteen months, or cycles of three hundred and sixty days."

It is certainly not to be doubted that the Mexican or Toltecan system of the distribution of time was extremely well digested, though at first view it appears rather intricate and perplexed; hence, we may infer with confidence it was not the work of a rude or an unpolished people. That, however, which is most surprising in their mode of computing time, and which will certainly appear improbable to readers who are ill informed with respect to Mexican antiquity, is that, having discovered the excess of a few hours in the solar above the civil year, they made use of intercalary days to bring them to an equality, but with the difference in regard to the method established by Julius Cæsar in the Roman calendar, that they did not interpose a day every four years, but thirteen days (making use even here of this favorite number) every fifty-two

* Vol. i, pp. 335, 336.

years, which produces the same regulations of time. At the expiration of the cycle they broke, as we shall mention hereafter, all the kitchen utensils, fearing that then also the fourth age, the sun and all the world were to be ended, and on the last night they performed the famous ceremony of the new fire. As soon as they were assured by the new fire that a new cycle, according to their belief, was granted to them by the gods, they employed the thirteen following days in supplying their kitchen utensils, in furnishing new garments, in repairing their temples and houses, and in making every preparation for the grand festivals of the new century.

These thirteen days were the intercalary days represented in their paintings by blue points; they were not included in the cycle just expired, nor in that which was just commencing, nor did they continue in them their periods of days which they always reckoned from the first day to the last day of the century.

When the intercalary days were elapsed they began the new cycle with the year I, Tochtli, and the day I, Cipactli, upon the twenty-sixth day of February, as they did at the beginning of the preceding cycle.

We would not venture to relate these particulars

if we were not supported by the testimony of Dr. Siguenza, who, "in addition to his great learning, his critical skill and sincerity, was the person who most diligently exerted himself to illustrate these points, and consulted with the best instructed Mexicans and Tezcocans, and studied their histories and paintings."

Some thirteen years since a missionary errand took us for the first time to Tula. We found a quiet little city, built largely of basaltic rock taken from the surrounding mountains or possibly from ancient ruins mostly buried beneath the surface. There was an attractive little plaza, with a bubbling fountain in the center. A noble cathedral, bearing the date of 1553, indicates the importance in which the Spanish invaders held the town three hundred and fifty years ago. "It is a magnificent building, with lofty groined ceiling, and with a collection of paintings that appear to possess great merit as well as antiquity." The ancient Tula River still encircles half the town, and a stone bridge arched, and with a parapet, carries the date 1772.

But on the right and left are evidences of greater antiquity than either bridge or cathedral can show. Some of these, as stated in a previous lecture, are in the very plaza, sacredly guarded by the government, and above the city, on a hill overlooking two valleys; on a ridge about a mile in length are the ruins of buildings erected perhaps as far back as the seventh and eighth centuries.

Prescott says of the settlement of the Toltecs here in 648, following the date given by Clavigero: "They fixed their capital at Tula, north of the Mexican valley, and the remains of extensive buildings were to be discerned there at the time of the conquest. The noble ruins of religious and other edifices are referred to this people, whose name, Toltec, has passed into a synonym for architect. Their shadowy history reminds one of those primitive races who preceded the ancient Egyptians in the march of civilization. After four centuries the Toltecs disappeared as silently and mysteriously as they came."*

Whatever of mystery may have surrounded their advent, their disruption as a nation is as circumstantially told, and is as authentic, as any history or tradition of that period. It is the old story, and the causes are such as have brought ruin to many a family and nation in the past. About the beginning of the eleventh century the seeds of disturbance were sown in the hitherto peaceful and prosperous kingdom of Tollan. Some Indians had found the squirrels sapping the maguey plant

* Prescott, vol. i, p. 8.

(agave), which produces at maturity great quantities of juice. From this originated the idea of scraping the heart of the ripe plant, allowing the juice to ferment, and thus inventing for themselves a drink which to this day is procured, prepared, and used in exactly the same way, known everywhere as the national beverage, pulque. Indeed, it is now raised in such quantities in the valley of Anahuac as to require a heavy railway train each day on three different railroads to supply the demand in the national capital alone. Whatever may be the profit accruing to railways from the traffic the beverage causes laziness, poverty, distress, and ruin to many a family that otherwise might be prosperous and happy. But the day is doubtless near at hand when this wonderful plant will be cultivated more for its fiber (which makes excellent cordage and superior paper) than for its sap. The Mexican pulque plant, like the palm of the Arabs and the bamboo of the East, serves many a purpose useful as well as ornamental.

On the discovery of pulque one of the nobles of Tollan went with his daughter to present a draught of the beverage to the king. So great was his delight with the giver and with the gift that she was ordered to return unattended by her father with more, and then she became a royal prisoner of the court. The illicit love of Tecpancaltzin, the monarch, brought with it its punishment. And when at last his natural son, Meconetzin, sat upon the throne the Toltecs were destroyed as a nation and the remnant of that ancient people scattered far and wide, the combined work of internal dissensions, famine, and an invading force from Jalisco. It was here that Quetzalcoatl, the great culture hero, the " Plumed Serpent," or " God of the Air," as he was sometimes called, and better known in the United States as the " Fair God," played an important rôle. Here may be seen the famous " Hill of Shouting," from whence he sent his summons and commands over the entire valley of Anahuac. Some say that he was a native of the East, and came across the great ocean. Some say that his miraculous birth was due to the fact that his mother swallowed a precious stone.* He has been claimed by nearly every nationality on earth. The following description by Professor Short is worthy of insertion here:

"From the distant East, from the fabulous Huehue Tlapallan, this mysterious personage came to Tollan, and became the patron, god, and high priest of the ancestors of the Toltecs. He is described as having been a white man, with a strong

* Chavero, p. 372.

formation of body, broad forehead, large eyes, and flowing beard. He wore a miter on his head, and was dressed in a long white robe reaching to his feet and covered with red crosses.. In his hand he held a sickle. His habits were ascetic ; he never married, was most chaste and pure in his life, and is said to have endured penance in a neighboring mountain, not for its effects upon himself, but as an example to others. Some have here found a parallel for Christ's temptation. He condemned sacrifices, except of fruits and flowers, and was known as god of peace ; for when addressed on the subject of war he is reported to have stopped his ears with his fingers.

"Quetzalcoatl was skilled in many parts, having invented gem cutting and metal casting. He furthermore originated letters and invented the Mexican calendar. The legend which describes the latter states that the gods, having made men, thought it advisable that their creatures should have some means of reckoning time and of regulating the order of religious ceremonies. Therefore two of these celestial personages, one of them a goddess, called Quetzalcoatl to counsel with them, and the three contrived a system which they recorded on tables, each bearing a single sign. That sign, however, was accompanied with all necessary explanations of its meaning. It is noticeable that the goddess was assigned the privilege of writing the first sign, and that she chose a serpent as her favorite symbol.

"Some accounts represent that Hueman was the temporal king, or at least associated with Quetzalcoatl in the government, the latter occupying the priestly as well as the kingly office. Sahagun calls the associate ruler Vemac. At all events, Quetzalcoatl had an enemy, the deity Tezcatlipoca, whose worship was quite opposite in its character to that of Quetzalcoatl, being sanguine and celebrated with horrid human sacrifices. A struggle ensued in Tula (Tollan) between the opposing systems, which resulted favorably to the bloody deity and the faction who sought to establish his worship in preference to the peaceful and ascetic service of Quetzalcoatl.

"Tezcatlipoca, envious of the magnificence enjoyed by Quetzalcoatl, determined upon his destruction. His first appearance at Tula was in the rôle of a great ball player, and Quetzalcoatl, being very fond of the game, engaged to play with him, when, suddenly, he transformed himself into a tiger, occasioning a panic among the spectators, in which great numbers were crowded over a precipice into a river, where they perished. Again the vicious god appeared at Tula. This time he presented himself at the door of Quetzalcoatl's palace in the guise of an old man, and asked permission of the servants to see his master. They attempted to drive him away, saying that the god was ill. At last, because of his importunities, they obtained leave to admit him. Tezcatlipoca entered, and, seeing the sick deity, asked about his health, and announced that he had brought him a medicine which would ease his body, compose his mind, and prepare him for the journey which fate had decreed that he must undertake.

"Quetzalcoatl received the sorcerer kindly, inquiring anxiously as to the journey and the land of his destiny. His deceiver told him that the name of the land was Tollan Tlapallan, where his youth would be renewed, and that he must visit it without delay. The sick king was moved greatly by the words of the sorcerer, and was prevailed upon to taste the intoxicating medicine which he pressed to his lips. At once he felt his malady healed, and the desire to depart fixed itself in his mind. 'Drink again!' exclaimed the old sorcerer; and again the god king pressed the cup to his lips and drank till the thought of departure became indelible, chained his reason, and speedily drove him a wanderer from his palace and kingdom. Upon leaving Tula, driven from his kingdom by the vicious enmity of Tezcatlipoca, he ordered his palaces of gold and silver and turquoise and precious stones to be set on fire. The myriads of rich-plumed songsters that made the air of the capital melodious with song accompanied him on his journey, pipers playing on pipes preceded him, and the flowers by the way are said to have given forth unusual volumes of perfume at his approach. After journeying one hundred leagues southward he rested near a city of Anahuac, under a great tree, and, as a memorial of the event, he cast stones at the tree, lodging them in its trunk. He then proceeded still further southward, in the same valley, until he came to a mountain two leagues distant from the city of Mexico. Here he pressed his hands upon a rock on which he rested, and left their prints imbedded in it, where they remained visible down to a very recent date. He then turned eastward to Cholula, where he was received with greatest reverence. The great pyramid was erected to his honor. With his advent the spirit of peace settled down upon the city. War was not known during his sojourn in it. The reign of Saturn repeated itself. The enemies of the Cholulans came with perfect safety to his temple, and many wealthy princes of other countries erected temples to his honor in the city of his choice.

"Here the silversmith, the sculptor, the artist, and the architect, we are led to believe, from the testimony of both tradition and remains, flourished under the patronage of the grand god king. However, after twenty years had elapsed that subtle, feverish draught received from the hands of Tezcatlipoca away back in Tula, like an old poison in the veins, renewed its power. Again his people, his palaces, and his pyramidal temple were forsaken, that he might start on his long and final journey. He told his priests that the mysterious Tlapallan was his destination, and, turning toward the east, proceeded on his way until he reached the sea at a point a few miles south of Vera Cruz. Here he bestowed his blessing upon four young men who accompanied him from Cholula, and commanded them to go back to their homes, bearing the promise to his people that he would return to them and again set up his kingdom among them. Then, embarking in a canoe made of serpent skins, he sailed away into the east.

"The Cholulans, out of respect to Quetzalcoatl, placed the government in the hands of the recipients of his blessing. His statue was placed in a sanctuary on the pyramid, but in a reclining position, representing a state of repose, with the understanding that it shall be placed upon its feet when the god returns.

"When Cortez landed they believed their hopes realized, sacrificed a man to him, and sprinkled the blood of the unhappy victim upon the conqueror and his companions."*

Most historians content themselves simply with stating at this period of events that toward the close of the existence of the Toltec power Anahuac was overrun by the incursions of a fierce and dreaded people, the Chichimecs. However, the origin, migration, and subsequent history of these mysterious people, of whom the Indians of Mexico still freely talk, is certainly worthy of a few moments' notice. While our information concerning their origin is not as complete as we could wish, yet it is quite evident that they were neighbors of the Toltecs in Huehue Tlapallan and, it would appear, had been in constant dread of them before and during the migrations.

We further find that their primitive land or home was called Amaquemecan; of its exact situation, Clavigero says, we are ignorant, and yet he locates it somewhere in North America, "like the north of Europe, the nursery of the human race. From both in swarms there issued numerous nations to people the countries in the south." †

---

* *North Americans of Antiquity*, p. 267, *et seq.;* also *Mexico Á Traves de los Siglos*, vol. i, pp. 272-274.   † Vol. i, p. 119.

Torquemada locates it six hundred miles to the north of the modern city of Guadalajara, which would bring it below the Texas border; possibly he meant leagues. Both he and Ixtlilxochitl represent the Chichimecs as pursuing and annoying the Toltecs in all their wanderings. Perhaps this is not literally true, but it does appear that they reached the borders of Anahuac soon after the Toltecs, possibly within eleven years. It also appears that early in the eighth century the Toltecs consented as a peace offering to accept a Chichimec prince for their king, but with the express condition that the Toltecs should always be a free people and be in no way tributary to the Chichimecs.

At first they doubtless spoke, as Pimentel asserts,* a language distinct from the Nahua nations, but subsequently adopted the Nahua tongue, on the principle asserted by the French linguist Balbi: "It is not the language of the conquering people that invariably dominates, but that which is most regular and cultured." † Pimentel further says that the language of the Chichimecs was not only once distinct from the Nahua, and "that these people came under the civilizing influences of the Toltecs during their golden age, but in their declining pe-

* Vol. i, chap. iii, Epstein edition of 1874.
† Quoted by Short.

riod availed themselves of the opportunity of possessing their country and advanced civilization."

If the Chichimecs and Toltecs were neighbors when the latter lived in Huehue Tlapallan, we might naturally look for some light on that disputed locality in the Chichimecan annals; but here again we are disappointed. Amaquemecan is the only name we find applied to their primitive home or history. Mr. Bancroft, after years of arduous research, declares that "there seems to be absolutely nothing to indicate whether Amaquemecan was in the north or south." Spanish authors all agree in the direction, though they disagree on the locality, assigning places all the way between Zacatecas, in Mexico, and as far north as Alaska. It also seems probable that the great original Nahua empire, whether it is named Huehue Tlapallan, Tamoanchan, Tollan, or Amaquemecan, was the Chichimecan empire; that is, that the Toltecs or revolting branch constituted but a small portion of the Chichimecan or Nahua people. At least so Mr. Bancroft and several other historians think.*

But, reverting to our story, we find the Chichimecs arriving in considerable numbers at Tollan (Tula) eighteen months after leaving Amaquemecan under command of Xolotl, according to Clavigero, in 1170,

* Bancroft, vol. v, p. 220.

though Lord Kingsborough puts it much earlier,* and Chavero shows clearly that they reached the valley of Mexico as early as 635. On arrival they found that the splendor of the ancient capital had departed, "its streets deserted and overgrown with vegetation, its magnificent temples and palaces were in ruins, and desolation reigned where so lately had been the hum and bustle of a mighty metropolis." After leaving some of his people in this place, which he considered too important to entirely abandon, notwithstanding its ruinous condition, he continued his march to Lake Xaltocan, where the people lived for some time in caves until they built the town of Xoloc, which still exists and bears the name of this nomadic chief from the north. About this time they are said to have numbered three million two hundred and two thousand men and women, children not included. Cempoala and other towns were founded, and finally Xolotl took up his permanent residence near the present modern town of Tezcoco. On the sides of the mountains overlooking this magnificent valley I have walked and have ridden over acres of ruins, destroyed, perhaps at first, by foreign invaders, and buried later by washes from the mountains or eruptions from the adjacent snow-capped Ixtaccihuatl and Popocatepetl,

* *Mexico Á Traves de los Siglos*, vol. i, p. 353.

which seem indeed "to kiss the firmament," and which form a most glorious background for the whole country. No wonder Xolotl tarried here. Never did earthly king find a more inspiring or a grander spot to plant a throne. After him reigned Xolotl II, and, as in the case of his father (or uncle), many smaller tribes seemed glad to be affiliated with this growing and prosperous kingdom.

At Culhuacan, Chapultepec, Quauhtitenco, and other centers friendly tribes were ruled over by lords, while at Cholula two priests held the reins of government, all of whom recognized the supremacy of Xolotl II. Representatives were dispatched to the four quarters and in time returned, bringing news of many settlements as far south as Coatzacoalcos, Tehuantepec, and even Guatemala. The remnants of the Toltecs in Anahuac offered no opposition, and the king proceeded to divide the land among his nobles, giving to each a definite section, with instructions to establish a central city to be named, in each case, after its founder. This, doubtless, accounts for what in some histories seems a multiplicity of nations.

The country thus divided reached the gulf coast, and it is said to have been over two hundred leagues in circumference. The heart of this ancient empire is to-day the very heart of the Methodist Mission;

and where once roved the half-naked hunter and semicivilized princes, some two or three score of our itinerants, "clothed in their right mind," under the orders of " the King of kings," are marching to sure and certain conquest for a kingdom which shall, unlike these of which we have been speaking, endure when the sun and moon no longer shine.

Anything like a complete history of the Chichimecs and their affiliated tribes, their wars and conquests, their successes and rebuffs, would require as much space as is allowed for this entire course of lectures. The student is respectfully referred to Bancroft's, to Short's, to Clavigero's, and to Lord Kingsborough's valuable works, from all of which we learn that the Chichimecan empire lasted from the twelfth century down to the year 1521 A. D., during which time they had eleven lawful kings and two usurpers upon the throne. After this latter date it became a part of the Mexican kingdom. Before dismissing the subject, however, the following brief account of their manners and customs, from one of Mexico's most reliable historians, may be of interest:

" The character of the Chichimecs, as is shown by their history, was very singular, as a certain degree of civilization was blended with many traits of bar-

barism. They lived under the command of a sovereign, and the chiefs and governors deputed by him, with as much submission as is usual among the most cultivated nations.

"There were distinctions between the nobility and commonalty, and the plebeians were accustomed to reverence those whose birth, merit, or favor with the prince raised them above other ranks. They dwelt in communities together, in places composed, as we may imagine, of poor huts; but they neither practiced agriculture nor those arts which accompany civil life. They lived only on game and fruits and roots which the earth spontaneously produced. Their clothing was the rough skins of the wild beasts they took in prey, and their arms no other than the bow and arrow. Their religion was reduced to the simple worship of the sun, to which pretended divinity they offered herbs and flowers which they found springing in the fields. With respect to their customs, they were certainly less displeasing and less rude than those to which the genius of a nation of hunters gives birth." *

The arrival of the Nahuatlaca tribes about this time deserves special notice. They came in different numbers, at different times, and under a variety

* Clavigero, vol. i, p. 120.

of names. Their original home was Aztlan, which Bourbourg locates in California; Prescott, Gondra, and Humboldt, "north of 42° north latitude" (Oregon, perhaps); Clavigero says, "north of the Colorado River;" the more recent school of Americanists gives it a southern location; while Father Duran, after locating it in Florida and asserting that his conclusions cannot be doubted, like all his contemporaneous authors, reverently adds, "Although in all I submit myself to the correction of the holy Catholic Church." *

Further along in his History this same author tells us how the royal chronologist, the aged Cueuhcoatl, described Aztlan to the elder Moctezuma when summoned to the court for this purpose. He replied to the emperor's question as follows:

"Our fathers dwelt in that happy and prosperous place which they called Aztlan, which means 'whiteness.' In this place there is a great mountain in the middle of the water, which is called Culhuacan, because it has the point somewhat turned over toward the bottom, and for this cause it is called Culhuacan, which means 'crooked mountain.'

"In this mountain were some openings or caves or hollows where our fathers and ancestors lived for many years; there, under this name Mexitin and

* *Historia de las Indias*, vol. i, p. 9.

Aztec, they had much repose; there they enjoyed a great plenty of ducks; of all species of marine birds and water fowls; enjoyed the song and melody of birds with yellow crests; enjoyed many kinds of large and beautiful fish; enjoyed the freshness of trees that were upon those shores, and fountains inclosed with elders and savins (junipers) and alder trees, both large and beautiful. They went about in canoes, and made furrows in which they planted maize, red peppers, tomatoes, beans, and all kinds of seed that we eat."*

The causes which impelled their exodus from such a delightful country can only be conjectured; but it is likely that they were driven out by a more powerful people. The native tradition relates that a bird was heard for many days repeating the word "Tihui, tihui," which means, "Let us go, let us go." With the same bird still singing in the forests of Mexico his melancholy "Tihui, tihui," it is difficult to persuade the descendants of these primitive races that old Huitzitin and Tecpatzin, wisest among the Nahuatlaca chiefs, did not receive a message from the gods directing their people to seek a new home.

After twenty-six years they reached Chicomoztoc, the famous "seven caves," which is regarded by Clavigero to be twenty miles south of the modern

*Historia de las Indias, vol. i, p. 219.

town of Zacatecas, where still exist the ruins of some great edifice. Seven tribes at least were centered, at one time, in Chicomoztoc, though some authors add the names of eight others.* Of the seven we will take time to mention only two, the two which eventually rose to great political importance. We refer to the Tlascalans, who founded a small though independent republic, and the Aztecs, " whose empire has been the wonder of students of antiquity and subject of histories as romantic as the purest fiction."

The first named, the Tlascalans, on arrival at Anahuac, established at Poyauhtlan, on the eastern shore of Lake Tezcoco. After they grew in numbers and attempted to usurp the lands of neighboring tribes, they so stirred up the latter as to cause three or four of them to make an alliance and to march against the Tlascalans. Being driven from the valley, part of them obtained permission to settle in Tollantzingo and in Quauhchinanco, while more than half of them found their way to Cholula, where they dislodged the Olmecs and Xicalancas. Soon after, however, the jealousy of neighboring tribes gave them trouble, and they were obliged to seek anew the protection of the Chichimecan king, and by the aid of their allied forces they came off

* Bancroft, vol. v, p. 307.

victorious. After a declaration of peace they fortified themselves in a permanent home. On their north and south rose nature's great bulwarks, the precipitous mountains, on their west they dug a great trench, and on their east built a high wall six miles in length, reaching completely across their territory from mountain to mountain. Within this small inclosure have lived the warlike and courageous Tlascalans during all these centuries, ever jealous of their honor and liberty. For a long time, and in spite of all opposition, they upheld the splendor of their little republic, until, at length, in confederacy with the Spaniards, they marched against their ancient rivals, the Mexicans, and in some measure shared a common ruin. Yet, though part of the Mexican federation, they retain many of their distinctive peculiarities, and their ancient republic is now known as the State of Tlascala. The meaning of the word is "a place of bread," and derives its origin from the great abundance of maize produced on its soil.

Some idea of the bravery of these noble Indians may be had from a circumstance connected with their early history. Since the time of the first Moctezuma all Mexican kings treated the Tlascalans as enemies. Strong garrisons were maintained along the frontiers of Tlascala so as to prevent trade with other tribes,

EARLY MEXICANS AND THEIR HISTORY. 155

and especially with the coast. Finding themselves thus deprived of the source of the necessaries of life, the Tlascalans sent a complaint to the Mexican court. The Mexicans, exalted by their prosperity, replied "that the King of Mexico was lord of all the world, and all mortals were his vassals,"* and as such the Tlascalans should render him obedience and pay him tribute ; otherwise their city would be sacked, they should perish, and their country be inhabited by another people.

To this arrogant answer the ambassador replied : " Most powerful lords, Tlascala owes you no submission, nor have the Tlascalans ever acknowledged any prince with tributes since their ancestors left the countries in the north to inhabit this land. They have always preserved their liberty, and, being unaccustomed to the slavery to which you pretend to subject them, rather than submit to your power they will shed more blood than their fathers shed in the famous battle of Payauhtlan." Without the alliance of such a people the Spanish conquest would have been impossible to Cortez.

The last of these migrating tribes from the north to reach the valley of Anahuac was the Aztec. They left Aztlan with the Nahuatlaca tribes, but remained longer in Chicomoztoc than the others, so

* Vol. i, p. 291.

that they did not reach Chapultepec till toward the close of the twelfth century, nearly four hundred years before the conquest. Perhaps no point of primitive Mexican history has given origin to greater discussion than the line of march followed by the Aztecs in their journey from Aztlan to Anahuac. Mr. Bancroft says: "It is utterly useless to attempt its clearing up, and I dispose of the whole matter by simply presenting in a note the dates and successive halting places attributed to this migration by the principal authorities." The time required to read his extended note is more than we can allow here.*

Perhaps Clavigero's plan is as correct as any, and as it has the virtue of being shorter than others we insert it here. It is as follows:

"The Aztecs left Aztlan in 1160, crossed the Colorado River, stayed three years at Huecolhuacan, went east to Chicomoztoc, where they separated from the Nahuatlaca tribes, then to Coatlicamac, and reached Tula in 1196, remaining nine years; then spent eleven years in different places, reached Zumpanco in 1216, remaining seven years, then Tizajocan, Tolpetlac, Tepejacac, and Chapultepec in 1245 during Nopaltzin's reign."†

* *Native Races*, vol. v, pp. 322–324.
† Clavigero, vol. i, pp. 150–156.

They had not been long on their journey till their religious tendency asserted itself. So they made a wooden image to represent Huitzilopochtli, the tutelar deity of the nation. They then made a chair of reeds and rushes in which to carry the image, and which they called Teoicpalli, or " chair of God." Four priests at a time were to carry him on their shoulders, and they were called Teotlamocazque, " servants of God," and the act itself was called Teomana, that is, " to carry God on one's back."

Mr. Bancroft * says that this Teoicpalli was a holy box, such as was used among the Etruscans and Egyptians, the Greeks and the Romans, in Ilium, among the Japanese and among the Mongols. In America the Cherokees are also found with such an ark. Wherever the Aztecs halted for some time during their wanderings they erected an altar or a sacrifice mound to their god, upon which they placed this god's litter with the image, which ancient observation they kept up in later times in their temples. By its side they erected a movable tent, *tabernaculum*, in the open country, as is customary among nomadic peoples, such as the Mongols. All of which reminds us of the ark of the covenant carried by the Levites, and the tabernacle in the wilderness.

* *Native Races*, vol. iii, p. 303.

Just after leaving Chicomoztoc and prior to reaching Tula a quarrel divided the tribe into two factions, so much so that they finally became perpetual rivals. Tradition says that the quarrel arose over two bundles which miraculously appeared in their camp. On examining one bundle it was found to contain an emerald of extraordinary size and beauty. The other was found to contain nothing but two pieces of wood. The party opening the first bundle called themselves Tlaltelulcas, and considered themselves the more fortunate, while the other faction, with the two pieces of wood, called themselves henceforth Mexicans, and were supposed to be the unfortunate ones. But when Huitziton made known to them a novel process of producing fire by rubbing two sticks together (an invention ever after prized by these people) they concluded that science and industry were preferable even to beauty or nobility as typified by the emerald.

Another legend oft quoted, and which has left its perpetual sign on the Mexican escutcheon, will bear repeating here: Not long after the event just referred to another mystery occurred in the camp. Their aged high priest, Huitziton, died or suddenly disappeared during the night. The next morning the report was everywhere circulated by his fellow-priests that he had taken his place among the gods,

EARLY MEXICANS AND THEIR HISTORY. 159

and that on his arrival there he was assured by the great Tetzuah that, though dead, he would still "guide and rule them from on high" and "show unto them the land which I have chosen for them, where they will have a long and prosperous empire." Abbé Brasseur de Bourbourg adds to the speech, "Where they shall find a nopal growing alone on a rock in the midst of the waters, and on this nopal an eagle holding a serpent in his claws ; there they are to halt, there will be the seat of their empire, there will my temple be built." *

This story is still told to justify the location of the national capital on its present site. Our own famous Bishop Simpson, during his episcopal visit to our sister republic in 1873, saw everywhere this emblem of the eagle on the nopal struggling with the serpent ; and when invited one day to a banquet in the American Legation, having among the auditors of his after-dinner speech President Lerdo de Tejada, made the happy hit, comparing the eagles of the two sister republics, that the special difference between the American and the Mexican eagle was " that the latter, though still struggling with the serpent of tyranny which the former had crushed, would soon, like the former, be absolutely free."

After a most circuitous route the Aztecs came at

* *Native Races*, vol. v, p. 327.

last to their journey's end. And when we remember that they were in quest of such a country as would afford them all the conveniences of life it is not to be wondered at that their migration was a very circuitous one. Nor is it surprising that in some cases they commenced to build palaces and temples, for they probably thought every stop would end their peregrination. Wherever they halted they raised an altar to their god, and in most cases representatives of their people remained behind, especially the aged and feeble and those weary of a wandering life. After Tula they came to Zumpanco, Tizayocan, Tepeyaca, Chapultepec, Mexicaltzingo, Ixtacalco, and other places, till at last they found a nopal growing on a stone, and on it the eagle struggling with a serpent. This place they named Tenochtitlan, the name by which Mexico city was known for ages. They immediately proceeded to erect a temple for their god Huitzilopichitli, at which time a human being was offered in sacrifice. One of the Mexicans went to hunt an animal for said sacrifice, but finding none he laid hands upon a Colhuan of a neighboring tribe, bound and dragged him to the temple, where "with great jubilee his heart was torn from his breast as he lay on the altar, and offered to their god." At this time the city was also called Mexico from the other of their gods, that is, the place or home of Mexitli. Such, in 1325, was the beginning of the city of Tenochtitlan, which in future times was to be the court of a great empire, and which in later years Clavigero was pleased to call " the largest and most beautiful city of the New World."

LECTURE V.

THE MOCTEZUMAS AND THE KING DAVID OF MEXICO.

LECTURE V.

THE MOCTEZUMAS AND THE KING DAVID OF MEXICO.

AT the close of the first quarter of the fourteenth century the situation in Mexico was about as follows: The Aztecs, or Mexicans, as they were afterward called, had planted their kingdom in Tenochtitlan within somewhat circumscribed territory, having for their central city, in the heart of the valley lakes, the spot where eagle, nopal, and serpent were to be found in mystic combination; a spot destined in future ages to be the site of Moctezuma's Halls, the seat of Spanish viceregal splendor, the brief American occupation under Scott, the turbulent court of French and Austrian usurpation, the theater alike of gayety, mourning, and the republican capital of a united and prosperous nation.

"The term Mexico has widely different meanings under different conditions. At first it signified only the capital of the Nahua nation, and it was five hundred years before it overspread the territory now known by that name. Mexico city was founded in 1325, and was called Mexico Tenochtitlan.

The latter appellation has been connected with Tenoch, the Aztec leader at that time, and with the sign of a nopal on a stone, called in Aztec respectively nochtli and tetl, the final syllable representing locality, and the first, Te, divinity or superiority. The word Mexico, however, was then rarely used, Tenochtitlan being the common term employed; and this was retained by the Spaniards for some time after the conquest, even in imperial decree, and in the official records of the city, though in the corrupt forms of Temixtitan, Tenustitan, etc. . . . Torquemada (i, 293) states distinctly that even in his time the natives never employed any other designation for the ancient city than Tenochtitlan, which was also the name of the chief and fashionable ward.

"Solis . . . is of the opinion that Mexico was the name of the ward, Tenochtitlan being applied to the whole city, in which case Mexico Tenochtitlan would signify the ward Mexico of the city Tenochtitlan.

"Gradually the Spanish records began to add Mexico to Tenochtitlan, and in those of the first provincial council, held in 1555, we find written Tenuxtitlan Mexico. . . . In the course of time the older and more intricate name disappeared, though the city arms always retained the symbolic nopal and stone. . . . A number of derivations have been given to the word Mexico, as Mextli, navel of the maguey, Metl-ico, place amidst the maguey; Mexico, on the maguey border; Mecitli, hare; Metzli, moon; Amexica or Mexica, you of the anointed ones. The signification spring or fountain has also been applied. But most writers have contented themselves by assuming it to be identical with the Mexi, Mexitl, or Mecitl, appellation of the war god Huitzilopochtli, to which has been added the Co, an affix implying locality; hence Mexico would imply the place or settlement of Mexica or Mexicans.

"This war god Huitzilopochtli, as is well known, was the mythic leader and chief deity of the Aztecs, the dominant tribe of the Nahua nation. It was by this august personage, who was also called Mexitli, that according to tradition the name was given them in the twelfth century, and in these words: 'Inaxcan aocmoamotoca ynamaz te ca ye am Mexica'— Henceforth bear ye not the name of Azteca, but Mexica. With this command they received the distinguishing mark of a patch of gum and feathers to wear upon their foreheads and ears."*

This little kingdom had an aristocratic form of government down to the year 1352, with twenty

* Bancroft, vol. ix, p. 12.

lords for rulers, the chief of them Tenoch. Stimulated by the example of their neighbors, the Chichimecs, the Tepanecs, and the Colhuas, they erected a monarchy with ambitious pretensions. Acamapitzin, famous and prudent, was chosen king, and after applying in vain to three adjoining realms they secured at last from Coatlinchan a noble prince for their young king as well as a queen for themselves. Their nearest neighbors, the Tlatelolcos, followed their example and erected a kingdom and invited Quaquauhpitzahuac, son of Atzcapozalco, of the Tepaneca nation, to accept the crown. This he did in 1353.

The Tezcocans across the lake were building up the Athens of Anahuac, for here was a seat of learning which has been the marvel of centuries. The kingdom of Acolhuacan was near by, but was too full of internal dissensions to have permanent existence, and when Chimalpopoca ascended the Mexican throne the Acolhuacan heard its death-knell as an independent nation, and Tezozomoc, the decrepit old king, "a monster of ambition, treachery, and injustice," ceased to live in 1422.

However, the Tezcocans and their civilization deserve more than a mere passing notice. Here flourished a civilization and center of learning which commands our admiration. We find the government divided into departments, such as a council of war, a council of finance, a council of justice, and a council of state. In each of these departments a certain number of citizens had voice and vote.

There is also a council of music, which, different from the meaning of its name, was devoted to science and art. Here the historian, the astronomer, the chronologer, and all other writers were obliged to submit their works before publication. This was exercising censorial power over the press with a vengeance. Mr. Prescott calls it " a general board of education for the country," and adds that the influence of this academy must have been most propitious to the capital, which became the nursery, not only of such sciences as could be compassed by the scholarship of the period, but of various useful and ornamental arts. Its historians, orators, and poets were celebrated throughout the country. Its archives, for which accommodations were provided in the royal palace, were stored with the records of primitive ages. Its idiom, more polished than the Mexican, was, indeed, the purest of all the Nahuatlac dialects, and continued, long after the conquest, to be that in which the best productions of the native races were composed. Tezcoco claimed the glory of being the Athens of the western world.

Perhaps the greatest wonder of Tezcoco and the

age of which we now speak was the emperor, Nezahualcoyotl, who lived in a royal white palace nearly three quarters of a mile in length and half a mile in width. He was frequently in the academy himself, now as critic, now as orator. He wrote so many songs that he is frequently referred to as the King David of Mexican history. Some of these have been translated by his direct descendant of the fourth generation, Ixtlilxochitl, and from them we gather something of the style. One of them ran like this:

> " Yo tocare cantando
> El Musico instrumento sonroso
> Tu de flores gozando
> Danza, y festeja a Dios que es poderoso ;
> O gozemos de esta gloria,
> Porque la humana vida es transitoria."

Dr. John Foster Kirk well says that the English poet, Herrick, has beautifully expressed this very common sentiment of the bard not only of Tezcoco, but of many other nations, in the following lines :

> " Gather the rosebuds while you may,
> Old time is still a-flying ;
> The fairest flower that blooms to-day
> To-morrow may be dying."

The evolution of the religious belief of the old king is intensely interesting. He was not married till late in life. Then, being disappointed in having no issue, he was led by the priests, though reluctanctly, to offer human sacrifices to the gods as his only hope. But though the altars again smoked with the blood of slaughtered captives it was all in vain. Then he declared : " These idols of wood and stone can neither hear nor feel, much less could they make the heavens, and the earth and man, the lord of it. These must be the work of the all-powerful unknown God, Creator of the universe, on whom alone I must rely for consolation and support."

After forty days of fasting and meditation in his rural palace of Tezcotzinco he publicly professed his new faith and labored to wean his subjects from their superstitions. "He built a temple in the regular pyramidal form, and in the summit a tower nine stories high, to represent the nine heavens; a tenth was surmounted by a roof painted black, and profusely gilded with stars on the outside and incrusted with metals and precious stones within. He dedicated this to 'the unknown God, the Cause of causes' (*Al Dios no conocido, causa de las causas.—* MS. de Ixtlilxochitl). It seems probable, from the emblem on the tower, as well as from the complexion of the verses, as we shall see, that he mingled with his reverence for the Supreme Being the astral worship which existed among the Aztecs. Various musical instruments were placed on the top of the tower, and the sound of them, accompanied by the ringing of a sonorous metal struck by a mallet, summoned the worshipers to prayers at regular seasons. No image was allowed in the edifice, as unsuitable to the 'invisible God,' and the people were expressly prohibited from profaning the altars with blood or any other sacrifices than that of the perfume of flowers and sweet-scented gums." *

His declining years were spent in the study of astronomy and "to meditation on his immortal destiny." His later verses show clearly that he turned for consolation "to the world beyond the grave." So he says: "All things on earth have their term, and in the most joyous career of their vanity and splendor their strength fails and they sink into the dust. All the round world is but a sepulcher, and there is nothing which lives on its surface that shall not be hidden and entombed beneath it. Rivers, torrents, and streams move onward to their destination. Not one flows back to its pleasant source. They rush onward, hastening to bury themselves in the deep bosom of the ocean. The things of yesterday are no more to-day, and the things of to-day will cease, perhaps, on the morrow. The cemetery is full of the loathsome dust of bodies once quickened by living souls who occupied thrones, presided over assemblies, marshaled

* Prescott's *Conquest*, vol. i, p. 89, Lippincott's edition.

armies, subdued provinces, arrogated to themselves worship, were puffed up with vainglorious pomp and power and empire.

"But these glories have all passed away like the fearful smoke that issues from the throat of Popocatepetl, with no other memorial of their existence than the record on the page of the chronicler. The great, the wise, the valiant, and the beautiful—alas! where are they now? They are all mingled with the clod, and that which has befallen them shall happen to us and to those that come after us. Yet, let us take courage, illustrious nobles and chieftains, true friends and loyal subjects, let us aspire to that heaven where all is eternal and corruption cannot come. The horrors of the tomb are but the cradle of the sun, and the dark shadows of death are brilliant light for the stars."*

Nezahualcoyotl died in 1470, at the age of seventy-two years, having ruled nearly half a century. He had done great things for his people by breathing into them new life and inspiration, extending their domains and lifting them high in the march of civilization. His closing hours, blessed by the tender embrace of his eight-year-old child and the committal to him of the crown, the final exhortation to his other children, the farewell to his ministers of state,

* Prescott's *Conquest*, vol. i, p. 89.

and other touching incidents, are graphically portrayed by Prescott and other historians—incidents that are most pathetic. But for that one foul blot of murder committed by him to obtain for wife one already betrothed to another he might, indeed, be considered "the greatest and best monarch who ever sat upon an Indian throne."

But to return to the neighboring nations. Dissensions continued for some time among these and other tribes in and adjoining the valley of Anahuac, till the Tepanecs were defeated and Atzcapotzalco was conquered. It was about this time that the first of the Moctezumas, the beginning of a glorious line, was born, rose to prominence and gave an example of civic bravery and of superstitious cowardice which is quoted with the passing centuries.

The Mexicans were at war with neighboring tribes which had united to dislodge them from their charmed and coveted Chapultepec. Moctezuma, not yet thirty years of age, had been put in charge of the forces marching under the triple insignia: the eagle, the nopal, and the serpent. The superior forces of the enemy had well-nigh crushed the Aztec, and it looked as though a retreat would be ordered. Just then, and a little before sunset, as reinforcements continued to swell the enemy's forces, dismay and complaint were widespread. Some even cried out, "What are we about, O Mexicans? Shall we do well in sacrificing our lives to the ambition of our king and our general?"

The king called a hasty council of princes and generals on the field of battle and propounded the question, "What shall we do?"

"What?" answered the noble young Moctezuma; "fight till death! If we die with our arms in our hands, defending our liberty, we will do our duty. If we survive our defeat we will remain covered with eternal confusion. Let us go, then; let us fight till we die."

King, nobles, officers, and soldiers caught the inspiration of the hour and exclaimed in one voice, "Let us die with glory." On they rushed; some to death, it is true, but as a body to complete and speedy victory. From that day to this the name of Moctezuma I has been a synonym for bravery. The mere name of Moctezuma, the gallant Tzin, on all festive occasions will now send a thrill of patriotism and of enthusiasm through the hearts of the indigenous people. Soon after the royal family of the Chichimecs was established on the throne of Acolhuacan. The monarchy of Tacuba was established. Then came the triple alliance of these two with the Mexican nation and the hero of Atzcapotzalco was anointed King Moctezuma I. Ere long the Tlatelolcos were brought into subjection. Moctezuma, pushing his victorious army on to the south, soon added to his crown the States of Huaxtepec, Juahtepec, Tepoztlan, Jacapichtla, Totolapan, Tlalcozanhtitlan, Chicapan, and many others. Then turning westward he met with similar success. After nine years he returned "with the spoils of many nations" to adorn the enlarged temple of Huitzilopochtli.

In 1446 came the great inundation, followed in 1448 and 1449 by the terrible famine. But in both these ordeals Moctezuma seemed as eminent as in times of war. In the first case as great skill was displayed by the Mexicans as was displayed by European engineers in a similar inundation under Spanish rule two hundred years later.

Then followed the conquest of the Mixtecas, and finally Moctezuma's army reached the gulf coast, victorious over everything, including the populous Olmec nation and only excepting that brave little Indian republic shut in by the mountains of Tlaxcala, unconquered even to the days of the Spaniards. Chalco, Tlalmanalco, and Ameca (in which last place one city lies buried beneath another) were soon embraced in the Mexican jurisdiction. So we find Moctezuma's empire on the east extending to the gulf; on the southeast, to the center of the Mixtec country; on the south, beyond Chilepan; on the west, to the valley of Toluca; on the northwest, to the heart of the Otomí country; and on the north, to the limit of the valley of Mexico. According to modern geography this included the States of Mexico, Puebla, Hidalgo, Guerrero, Vera Cruz, and western Oaxaca, with parts of Tamaulipas, San Luis Potosí, Queretaro, and Chiapas.

It seems impossible to ascertain the exact number of inhabitants of the country prior to the conquest. But native historians all claim that the country was much more thickly inhabited then than now. There is data, however, upon which to base such a claim. For we find that soon after the death of Moctezuma I the following provisions were needed annually to sustain the royal Acolhuacan family alone, namely, 318,519½ tons of corn, 178,360 tons of cocoanuts, 208 tons of red peppers, 44⅔ tons small peppers, 1,300 large baskets of salt, and 8,000 turkeys. Such a family could hardly be supported by a smaller nation than the Chichimecs, for whom were claimed three and a half millions. Certainly, then, we are not far out of the way in claiming ten millions for the central table-lands and as many more for the Western and Southern States and for Yucatan, where the Maya civilization was then flourishing. Eminent Mexican scholars will not admit of less than twenty-five million, and Humboldt estimates thirty million. To the shame of Spain be it said that the population of Mexico is less than half that number now.

The second Moctezuma, nephew of the first, began his reign in the last years of the fifteenth century. He was a brave general, a humble priest, a renowned astronomer, and "much revered for his gravity, his circumspection, and his religion. He was a man of a taciturn temper, extremely deliberate, not only in words, but also in his actions; and whenever he spoke in the royal council, of which he was a member, he was listened to with respect." When the news of his election from among a large number of legal candidates was published the allied kings seemed to vie with each other in doing him honor. Moctezuma himself, on being apprized of it, retired at once to the temple, and in order to simulate the humility with which he received the honor of his election set to work sweeping the pavement of the temple. From this humble pastime he was conducted by a numerous attendance to the palace and duly notified, with prolific flow of Aztec eloquence, of his election, in which election the official orator saw "how strong is the love which the omnipotent God bears to this nation" in giving a ruler of "no less fortitude than your invincible heart possesses and no less wisdom than that which in you we admire."

The newly elected king was moved to tears. Overcoming his emotion, he made fitting reply, listened quietly to the closing ceremonies, and then retired for four days of fasting in the temple, at the end of which he was reconducted in great state to the royal palace. He then marched against the Atlixchese, at that time rebels against the crown, and took enough prisoners for the sacrifice connected with his coronation. "On this occasion was displayed so much pomp of games, dances, theatrical representations, and illuminations, and with such variety and richness of tributes sent from the different provinces of the kingdom, that foreigners never known before in Mexico came to see it, and even the enemies of the Mexicans, namely, the Tlaxcalans and the Michicacanese, were present in disguise at the spectacle." *

As soon, however, as Moctezuma had the reins of government well in hand he began to develop great taste for display. Perhaps nothing will give a better idea of the strength and power of his kingdom than a description of his court. No one could enter the palace either to serve or confer without leaving his sandals at the door. No person could

* Clavigero, vol. i, p. 279.

appear before the king in anything like pompous dress; all persons on entering the hall of audience, and before speaking to the king, made three bows, saying at the first, "*Tlatoani*"—lord; at the second, "*Notlatosatzin*"—my lord; and at the third, "*Huitlatoani*"—great lord. They spoke low, and with bowed heads awaited the king's reply by means of his secretary, as if they awaited the voice of an oracle. On retiring the back was never turned on the throne.

The immense audience hall served also for a banqueting room. "The table was a large pillow, and his seat a low chair. The tablecloth, napkins, and towels were of cotton, but very fine, white, and always perfectly clean. The kitchen utensils were of the earthenware of Cholula; but none of these things ever served him but once, as immediately after he gave them to one of his nobles. The cups in which they prepared his chocolate and other drinks of the cocoa were of gold, or some beautiful seashell or naturally formed vessels curiously varnished. . . . He had gold plate, but it was only used on certain festivals in the temple. The number and variety of dishes at his table amazed the Spaniards who saw them. The conqueror Cortez says that they covered the floor of a great hall, and that there were dishes of every kind of game, fish, fruit, and herbs of the country. Three or four hundred noble youths carried this dinner in form, presented it as soon as the king sat down to the table, and immediately retired, and that it might not grow cold every dish was accompanied with its chafing dish. The king marked with a rod, which he had in his hand, the meats which he chose, and the rest were distributed among the nobles who were in the antechamber. Before he sat down four of the most beautiful women of his seraglio presented water to him to wash his hands, and continued standing all the time of his dinner, together with six of his principal ministers and his carver. As soon as the king sat down to table the carver shut the door of the hall, that none of the other nobles might see him eat. The ministers stood at a distance and kept a profound silence, unless when they made answer to what the king said. The carver and the four women served the dishes to him, besides two others who brought him bread made of maize baked with eggs. He frequently heard music during the time of his meal, and was entertained with the humorous sayings of some deformed men whom he kept out of mere state. He showed much satisfaction in hearing them, and observed that among their jests they frequently pronounced some important truth. When his dinner was over he took tobacco mixed with liquid amber, in a pipe or reed beautifully varnished, and with the smoke of it put himself to sleep. After having slept a little upon the same low chair he gave audience and listened attentively to all that was communicated to him, encouraged those who, from embarrassment, were unable to speak to him, and answered everyone by his ministers or secretaries. After giving audience he was entertained with music, being much delighted with hearing the glorious actions of his ancestors sung. At other times he amused himself with seeing various games played. . . . When he went abroad he was carried on the shoulders of the nobles in a litter covered with a rich canopy, attended by a numerous retinue of courtiers, and wherever he passed all people stopped with their eyes shut, as if they feared to be dazzled with the splendor of majesty. When he alighted from the litter to walk they spread carpets, that he might not touch the earth with his feet.

"The grandeur and magnificence of his palaces, houses of pleasure, woods, and gardens were correspondent to this majesty. The palace of his usual residence was a vast edifice of stone and lime which had twenty doors to the public square and streets, three great courts, in one of which was a beautiful fountain, several halls, and more than a hundred chambers. Some of the apartments had walls of marble and other valuable kinds of stone. The beams were of cedar, cypress, and other excellent woods, well finished and carved. Among the halls there was one so large that, according to the testimony of an eyewitness of veracity, it could contain three thousand people. Besides this palace he had others, both within and without the capital. In Mexico, besides the seraglio for his wives, there was lodging for all his ministers and counselors and all the officers of his household and court ; and also accommodation for foreign lords who arrived there, and particularly for the two allied kings.

"Two houses in Mexico he appropriated to animals: the one for birds which did not live by prey ; the other for birds of prey, quadrupeds, and reptiles. There were several chambers belonging to the first and galleries supported on pillars of marble, all of one piece. These galleries looked toward a garden, where, in the midst of some shrubbery, ten fishponds were formed, some of them of fresh water, for the aquatic birds of rivers, and others of salt water for those of the sea. In other parts of the house were all sorts of birds, in such number and variety as to strike the Spaniards with wonder, who could not believe there was any species in the world wanting to the collection. They were supplied with the same food which they fed upon while they enjoyed their liberty, whether seeds, fruits, or insects. For those birds which lived on fish only, the daily consumption was ten Castilian pesos of fish, which is more than three hundred Roman pounds. Three hundred men, says Cortez, were employed to take care of those birds, besides their physicians, who observed their distempers and applied timely remedies to them. Of these three hundred men some procured them their food, others distributed it, others took care of their eggs at the time of their incubation, and others picked their plumage at certain seasons of the year; for, besides the pleasure which the king took in seeing so great a multitude of animals collected together, he was principally careful of their feathers, not less for the sake of the famous mosaic images, . . . than of the works which were made of them. The halls and chambers of those houses were so many in number, as the conqueror above mentioned attests, that they could have accommodated two great princes with all their retinue. This celebrated house was situated in the place where at present the great Convent of St. Francis stands." *

This description might be continued at considerable length, but we pause here to remark that, in

* Clavigero, vol. i, p. 282.

the wonderful providence of God, on the very spot where stood this marvelous and extensive pleasure palace, and where later the Franciscan monks erected the magnificent convent which served them for over three hundred years, on this very spot, we repeat, to-day stands the handsome headquarters of the Methodist Episcopal Church in the land of Moctezuma.

Just outside the city the emperor had magnificent gardens, such as Chapultepec, Peñon, and other places, kept in exquisite order and neatness. In these, as well as in his palaces, gorgeous baths abounded, which were his daily delight. Four regal robes were donned every day and never used a second time, but handed down to the nobles or gallant soldiers who had distinguished themselves in battle. Goldsmiths, workers in mosaic sculptors, painters, and numerous other artists and artisans were kept constantly employed under his direction. He was attentive to the execution of law and order and an implacable enemy to idleness. Though arrogant and proud and excessively severe in punishment, he constantly did many things to gain the love of his subjects. Among his more noble public works was the perfect equipment of Colhuacan as a grand asylum for the aged and infirm whose every want was supplied from the royal exchequer. Nor was his zeal for religion less conspicuous than his other traits. He built several temples and was greatly devoted to their ceremonies, but at the same time his mind was perpetually enslaved by the fear of the auguries and pretended oracles of false divinities. Indeed, nearly every public event during the last days of Moctezuma was clothed with a mysterious significance, "every unusual phenomenon of nature, every accident, every illness, every defeat in battle, failure of crops, excessive heat or cold, rain or snow, thunder and lightning, shooting star or comet, earthquake or eclipse, each and all portended evil to the Atzec empire—evil which some seem even at this time to have connected with the olden predictions of Quetzalcoatl respecting the coming of a foreign race to take possession of the country." Monarch, nobles, and priests seem to have been kept in a constant state of alarm. Part of this condition of things, as described by historians, is, doubtless, due to the superstitious minds of the people, and in part is the result of the inventive imagination of native historians, colored, perhaps, in after years, by the first Catholic fathers who visited Mexico.

It is also believed by some that rumors had reached the ears of Moctezuma and his companions of the presence of Europeans on the

American coasts. The Spaniards were already in the Antilles, and Columbus had coasted Central America. Some knowledge of these facts had doubtless been carried by Aztec traders from the gulf to the table-lands.

Among the mysterious omens recorded by historians, in all sobriety, were a great comet with three heads which appeared about 1515, and "a wonderful pyramidal light" in the east, visible for forty days, similar to the aurora borealis. The King of Tezcoco was awed and subdued, but Moctezuma was so defiant and angry that Father Duran says he "strangled many of his sorcerers for their unfavorable interpretation of the signs and their failure to avert evil omens."

Soon after it is recorded that the "towers of Huitzilopochtli's temple took fire in a clear night without apparent cause and were reduced to ashes." And another temple was struck by lightning. Torquemada, Clavigero, and Betancourt all declare that Moctezuma's sister, Papantzin, who had been spirited away, was believed by all to have risen from the dead and appeared to her royal brother with the story of a new and powerful people who were to possess the land and bring with them a new religion. The matter of religion was probably added by the "ever truthful" Church writers. However, it is claimed that she survived the arrival of the Spaniards, and Clavigero says: "She was the first who in 1524 received the sacred baptism in Tlaltelolco, and was called from that time Doña Maria Papantzin."*

On the north side of the present city of Mexico, and about half a mile from our Mission quarters, stands a chaplet which marks the spot where the princess is said to have been baptized.

Time and space beyond our control would be needed to give anything like an adequate account of the other nations and tribes outside the central plateau of Mexico. But these were so related, before and after the conquest, with affairs centering in Anahuac, that we deem the following picture, drawn by Mr. Bancroft, of things as they appeared in 1519, to be of interest and to show the most extraordinary combination of circumstances that made it possible for a small invading army to overthrow an immense aboriginal empire, and hence we reproduce it:

"The power known as Aztec, since the formation of the tripartite alliance not quite a century before under the Acolhua, Mexican, and Tepanec kings, had gradually extended its iron grasp from its center about the lakes to the shores of either ocean;

*Clavigero, vol. i, p. 369.

and this it had accomplished wholly by the force of arms, receiving no voluntary allegiance.

"Overburdened by taxation, oppressed and insulted by royal governors, Aztec tribute gatherers, and the traveling armies of Tlatelulca merchants, constantly attacked on frivolous pretexts by bloodthirsty hordes who ravaged their fields and carried away the flower of their population to perish on the Mexican altars, the inhabitants of each province subjected to this degrading bondage entertained toward the central government of the tyrants on the lakes feelings of the bitterest hatred and hostility, only awaiting an opportunity to free themselves, at least to annihilate their oppressors. Such was the condition of affairs and the state of feeling abroad; at home the situation was more critical. The alliance which had been the strongest element of the Aztec power was now practically broken up; the ambitious schemes of Moctezuma had alienated his firmest ally, and the stronger part of the Acolhua force was openly arrayed against him under Ixtlilxochitl at Otompan, leagued with the Tlascaltec leaders for the overthrow of the Mexican power. It is probable that the coming of the Spaniards retarded rather than precipitated the united attack of the Acolhuas and the outside provinces on Moctezuma. But again, to meet the gathering storm, the Mexican king could no longer count on the undivided support of his own people; he had alienated the merchants, who no longer, as in the early days, did faithful duty as spies, nor toiled to enrich a government from which they could expect no rewards; the lower classes no longer deemed their own interests identical with those of their sovereign. Last, but far from least among the elements of approaching ruin, was the religious sentiment of the country. The reader has followed the bitter contentions of earlier times in Tollan and Culhuacan, between the rival sects of Quetzalcoatl and Tezcatlipoca. With the growth of the Mexican influence the bloody rites of the latter sect had prevailed under the auspices of the god Huitzilopochtli, and the worship of the gentler Quetzalcoatl, though still observed in many provinces and many temples, had, with its priests, been forced to occupy a secondary position. But the people were filled with terror at the horrible extent to which the latter kings had carried the immolation of human victims; they were sick of blood and of the divinities that thirsted for it; a reaction was experienced in favor of the rival deities and priesthood.

"And now, just as the oppressed subjects of priestly tyranny were learning to remember with regret the peaceful teachings of the Plumed Serpent, and to look to that god for relief from their woes, their prayers were answered, Quetzalcoatl's predictions were apparently fulfilled, and his promised children made their appearance on the eastern ocean. The arrival of Cortez at this particular juncture was, in one sense, most marvelous; but in his subsequent success there is little to be wondered at; nor is it strange that the oppressed Nahuas received almost with outstretched arms the ministers of the new faith thus offered them by the Spaniards." *

Not only the people but the country, with its wonderful resources, had drawn attention, for it was a land with varied climates, producing between the hot coast lands and the frigid zone, nestling just beneath the perpetual snow lines of mountains rising above the clouds, nearly every known fruit and cereal.

From the time of the conquest down to 1880 official records show that Mexican gold mines produced $120,000,000, and the silver mines, $2,999,-000,000 making a total of $3,111,000,000 worth of these two precious metals. But if to this we could add what was smuggled out of the country, and then the iron, the copper, lead, and amber output, the opals, onyx, and other valuable stones, rich dye

* Bancroft, vol. v, pp. 481, 482.

and cabinet woods, and many other products, we would get some idea of the worth of the prize for for which Spain was striving. It must have been this anticipation which led Cortez, on landing for the first time on this western world, to say to the Governor of Cuba, who offered him an emigrant's portion of land, "I came to get gold, not to till the soil like a peasant." This golden inspiration, too, manifested itself again and again, and, in spite of the repeated protests of a few of the better Spanish friars like Las Casas, the worthy Bishop of Chiapas, survived in the great majority of the conquerors. The pulse of European life beat very high in those days. Its feverish character contributed to multiply adventurers by the score and hundreds. Indeed, the condition of things on the continent in the early part of the sixteenth century was responsible for the conquest. In order to refresh our minds, and at the same time to give an idea of the way Mexican authors look back upon the scene, let us quote from General Vicente Riva Palacios, at present Mexico's worthy ambassador to Spain. In the introduction to his portion of *Mexico Through the Ages* * he speaks as follows of those times in Europe:

"It was the age of combat of all against all. Religious, political, social, literary, and scientific

* Vol. ii, p. 3.

struggles ; discoveries and conquests of unknown lands ; reforms in customs, in legislation, in religion, in philosophy—all, all were attracted and attempted by that age which, by means of a convulsive and sanguinary evolution, prepared the geography of the world and the conditions of minds to receive the seeds of a modern civilization.

"War covered the face of the old continent. Spain and France bathed in blood the plains of Pavia, where death, in the embrace of two conflicting armies, harvested the flower of the nobility that clustered about Francis I, armies impelled by the jealousies of two haughty and ambitious sovereigns, rather than by the love of country.

"Italy, the standard-bearer of civilization in Europe—Italy, with its poets and its politicians, its artists and its philosophers, shuddered sore and stricken under the severest revolutions that had clouded its history. . . . Meanwhile, the Republican school arose in Venice, led by Durantino, Cantarini, and Garinberti, and minds tossed to and fro and consciences were stirred. Then the statesmen and the warriors of Italy deployed their rhetoric and their arms, alike active on both sides; cities were captured by assault or by surprises, while foreign armies, with warlike movements, entered and left that classic land of art and history.

"The struggle between the common classes and the troops of the Emperor Charles V shook the new and virile monarchy born of the happy union of the knightly Ferdinand and the noble and poetic 'Isabel the Catholic.' . . . Noblemen wandered in terror through insurgent cities, while bishops sought refuge in the hospitals, as their palaces disappeared in smoke.

"The city of the Cæsars was taken by assault. The soldiery of the Constable of Bourbon, like the Godos of Alaric, entered to plunder, and the pope became the prisoner of Charles V, who at the same time ordered that prayer be made throughout all Christendom for the fate of the chief of the Catholic Church.

"The first sparks flew from the flames of religious war about to desolate Europe. In the name of the liberty of the human conscience, and in defiance of the successors of St. Peter, Luther fastened to the doors of the Wittenberg Cathedral his famous protest as a challenge, and from the Diet of Worms and the Confession of Augsburg rose the great edifice of religious reformation. Under the heat of that Reformation the Company of Jesus was born in the Catholic camp, and Henry VIII in England sealed with the blood of martyrs the birth of the Anglican Church, followed by the stakes fired in the

THE MOCTEZUMAS. 195

Netherlands by the Duke of Alba and the frightful massacre of the night of St. Bartholomew.

"Zwingle overturned Switzerland, Cranmer revolutionized England, while Knox in Scotland, Calvin in France, and Gustav Wasa in Sweden changed the order of things.

"From the fierce light that beat from that universal conflagration the sciences and the arts rescued giants who well could have baptized the age with their glorious names, had it not been the age of Charles V and Philip II, Luther and St. Ignatius de Loyola, Cortez and Don Juan of Austria—had the age not given birth to the conquest of America and to religious wars. However, therefrom irradiate the luminous faces of Raphael and Michael Angelo, Ariosto and Ulrich, Copernicus and Erasmus, Cardano and Tartaglia, Macchiavelli and Rabelais, Camden, Tasso and Cervantes, Shakespeare and Ercilla, Galileo, Kepler, and Bacon.

"Across that age of revolution, across that historic period, carrying upon his shoulders the terrible weight of two worlds, swept the son of Crazy Jane, the Emperor Charles V, probably the most powerful monarch that ever ruled in this world. Struggling with difficulties, which seemed insurmountable, in order to clasp the crown of Castile and Aragon, that young monarch, who reached

Spain almost a pretender, in a few years filled with his name a whole age and two worlds, introducing a great political revolution on earth; and under the sweeping shadow of his banners and among the turmoil of arms planting the germs of great nationalities which should in future divide up the world.

"The standards of the emperor floated triumphantly in Europe and in Asia, in Africa and in America. Before him bent obsequient alike the inhabitants of the Antilles and the haughty Spanish magnates, the keen Italian princes and the superb German lords. Among the captives were the Roman Pontiff, the King of France and the King of Navarre, the emperors of Mexico and of Peru, Muley-Azen, King of Tunis, and many of the New World sovereigns. The fate of the nations of both continents hung upon his decision, for one word from him sufficed to draw the swords of his great captains. When, wearied of glory and of struggle, of triumph and of disenchantment, he sought in the retirement of a cloistered cell a peace impossible to woo, he left upon the throne of Spain, like the haunting specter of his past glory and genius, the somber Philip II, upon whose domain the sun could not set, and who by artful and mysterious diplomacy sought to strengthen the conquests of his father, while on the fields of battle the descendants

THE MOCTEZUMAS. 197

of the Prophet of Mecca had torn from them even the hope of resumption of influence in Europe, while this monarch calmed the fears of terrorized Christianity, which had seen the crescent creep up over the city walls of Constantinople, that city consecrated by the sublime death of the last Constantine.

"In that great age, the age of stupendous achievements, the kings of Spain acquired by right of conquest, consecrated by Alexander VI, the rich and fertile dominions which in the world of Columbus received, by the will and word of Hernan Cortez, the name of New Spain."*

* The lecturer exhibited one of the first copies, in Latin, of the Bull of Alexander VI, by which he divided the western hemisphere between the Spanish and Portuguese. It is dated May 3, 1492.

14

LECTURE VI.

THE ARRIVAL OF THE SPANIARDS.

LECTURE VI.

THE ARRIVAL OF THE SPANIARDS.

HERNAN CORTEZ is regarded as the central figure of the Spanish conquest. True, other Spaniards had preceded him in the discovery of Mexico, but they had only coasted the gulf and never penetrated inland to any great distance. This real conqueror was born at Medellin, in the Province of Estremadura, Spain, in 1483—though Pizarro y Orellana, a zealous historian of the Church, publishes the remarkable coincidence " that Cortez came into the world the same day that that infernal beast, the false heretic, Luther, entered it." Mendieta says: " The same year that Luther was born in Eisleben, Hernan Cortez was born in Medellin, the first to disturb the world and put under the devil's banner many faithful ones whose fathers and grandfathers for long years were Catholics, and the second to bring into the pale of the Church infinite multitudes who for numberless years had been under the power of Satan wrapped up in vice and blind with idolatry." This would fix his birth in 1483, two years earlier than the more reliable historians give it.

Gomera, in his *History of Mexico*, page 4, tells us that Hernan was a sickly child, and would probably have died had not his faithful nurse, Maria de Estevan, secured the special protection of St. Peter in his behalf. It seems that, characteristic of the times, she drew lots from among the twelve apostles. The choice falling upon St. Peter she made him the patron saint of the youthful invalid, to whom she then offered special " masses and prayers, by which it pleased God to heal him."

Cortez's parents designed that he should study law, and for this purpose he went to Salamanca, a Spanish university of great renown. But student life did not fill the requirements of his restless spirit. After two years he returned to Medellin, devoting himself to sports and martial exercises. He became so impetuous, overbearing, and dissipated that his parents gladly consented to his going abroad as an adventurer. His first inclination was to go to Italy. But an illness resultant upon dissipation kept him bedridden till after the sailing of an expedition in which he had enlisted. His thoughts next turned to Hispaniola, where Ovando, a relative of his, was governor. He reached Santo Domingo in 1504, a youth of nineteen summers. The white dove spoken of by Prescott as lighting on the topmast of his vessel just prior to sighting land,

Pizarro y Orellana says was the Holy Spirit, which appeared in this form to guide an expedition "which was to redound so much to the spread of the Catholic faith and the Castilian monarchy."*

His reception by the governor was cordial, and he immediately received lucrative employment, but not sufficient to satisfy his ambition. Seven years later he accompanied Diego Velasquez to Cuba, where new employments and land grants soon made him a fortune. Though up to this time he had occupied comparatively humble positions in government service, still he had, as Robertson says, " displayed such qualities in several scenes of difficulty and danger as raised universal expectation, and turned the eyes of his countrymen toward him as one capable of performing great things. The turbulence of youth, as soon as he found objects and occupations suited to the ardor of his mind, gradually subsided, and settled into a habit of regular indefatigable activity. The impetuosity of his temper, when he came to act with his equals, insensibly abated, by being kept under restraint, and mellowed into a cordial, soldierly frankness. These qualities were accompanied with calm prudence in concerting his schemes, with persevering vigor in executing them, and with, what is peculiar to su-

* *Varones Ilustres*, p. 70.

perior genius, the art of gaining the confidence and governing the minds of men; to all which were added the inferior accomplishments that strike the vulgar and command their respect; a graceful person, a winning aspect, extraordinary address in martial exercises, and a constitution of such vigor as to be capable of enduring any fatigue." *

However, the young hero of the Spanish conquest had his weaknesses, and his career from that time to the final departure for Mexico was very checkered. A succession of difficulties with the lieutenant governor of Cuba resulted in his imprisonment, his escape, his second imprisonment, and his second escape. Finally, he effected a complete and permanent reconciliation, making a thrilling tale for both Prescott and Bancroft.

Cordova and Grijalva anticipated Cortez in reaching the Mexican shores, and though inferior in talents and fame to him, they were his superiors in honesty. Whether Velasquez knew this or not, as he instructed Cortez "to observe a conduct befitting a Christian soldier," is not stated. But subsequent events prove how lightly his instructions rested on his heart and conscience, while his love of gold never left him.

Cortez was also instructed to prohibit blasphemy,

* Robertson's *America*, p. 198.

THE ARRIVAL OF THE SPANIARDS. 205

licentiousness, and gambling among his men, and on no account to molest the natives, "but gently to inform them of the glory of God and of the Catholic king.* But Mohammed himself was not more cruel and relentless with his interlaced Koran and scimiter than was Cortez with the cross of Christ and sword of Toledo. A black banner of velvet, embroidered with the royal arms of Spain in gold, with blue and white flames surrounding a red cross, was made for the expedition, and upon it was inscribed the following: "Amici sequamur crucem, si nos habuerimus fidem in hoc signo vincemus"—"Friends, let us follow the cross, and under this sign, if we have faith, we shall conquer." † How different a translation did the great Constantine give to the heavenly vision, "In hoc signo vinces," and yet the opportunity was far greater for Cortez than for the first Christian emperor of Rome. Passing muster it was found that the expedition to Mexico contained 15 vessels, 110 mariners, 553 soldiers, 200 Indians from the island, several servant women, and 16 horses.

Cortez addressed his men in the following theatrical fashion: "I hold out to you a glorious prize, but it is to be won by incessant toil. Great things

---

* Bancroft's *Works*, vol. ix, p. 54.
† Prescott, vol. i, p. 118.

are achieved only by great exertions, and glory was never the reward of sloth. If I have labored hard and staked my all in this undertaking, it is for the love of that renown which is the noblest recompense of man. But if any among you covet riches more, be true to me, and I will be true to you and to the occasion, and I will make you masters of such as our countrymen have never dreamed of. You are few in number but strong in resolution; and, if this does not falter, doubt not but that the Almighty, who has never deserted the Spaniard in his contest with the unbeliever, will shield you, though encompassed by a cloud of enemies; for your cause is a just cause, and you are to fight under the banner of the cross. Go forward, then, with alacrity and confidence, and carry to a glorious issue the work so auspiciously begun."* Mass was said, the fleet was placed under the protection of St. Peter, the patron saint of Cortez, and they set sail on the 16th of February, 1519, to conquer an unknown people, and in doing so to write some of the bloodiest pages ever written in human history.

At the very outset of the conquest we find ourselves embarrassed by the greatly exaggerated chronicles of Spanish historians. For instance, after a short stop at the island of Cozumel, Cortez coasted

* Prescott, vol. i, p. 20.

THE ARRIVAL OF THE SPANIARDS. 207

along the shore of Yucatan and crossed the arm of the gulf until he entered the Tabasco River. There he landed on a little island called Punta de los Palmares. The natives resented their landing and a battle ensued. When we remember that Cortez only had a few hundred men in this expedition, it certainly seems strange to see Bernal Diaz claim that eight hundred Indians were killed in the first engagement, while Torquemada claims that one thousand fell. Cortez in his official dispatches says that forty thousand natives were drawn up in battle, and Bishop Las Casas gives thirty thousand souls as the modest number "cruelly slaughtered," and all this in a few hours by about five hundred Spaniards fighting under the disadvantages of a difficult landing and excessive tropical heat. This same spirit of exaggeration runs through the entire story of the conquest as written by the Spaniards. Unfortunately it has often misled our own flowery and enchanting Prescott.

It was at this time that Cortez manifested one of those memorable traits which so frequently characterized him in his relations to the people whom he had professedly come to Christianize. After the battle the bewildered natives sued for peace, and their overtures were accompanied by a propitiatory offering. To the first ambassadors Cortez answered with the following haughty reprimand: "Tell your master if he desires peace he must sue for it, and not send slaves." Next came an embassy of forty chiefs richly clad and walking in stately procession, followed by a file of slaves bearing presents. Bowing low " before the bearded assembly, and swinging before them the censer in token of reverence, the ambassador implored pardon and proffered submission. 'The blame is all your own,' said Cortez, with severity. The Indians acquiesced, though it puzzled them to know why they were to blame. Cortez informed them that the great king, his master, had sent him to scatter blessings, if they were found deserving; if not, to let loose upon them the caged lightning and the thunder which they carried. Whereat the gun charged for the occasion was fired, and the noise reverberated over the hills, the ball went crashing through the trees, the Indians fell prostrate with fear, and the noble Europeans were proud of their superiority." * This was but a sample of the tricks played upon the untutored Indian by these worthy Christian conquerors.

The natives were subdued, and, as the conquerors found that there was but little gold to demand, the precious metal being further inland, they proceeded to expound the doctrines of their faith, " to lay be-

* Bancroft's *Works*, vol. ix, p. 91.

fore them the truths of the Gospel they had come so far to bring." An altar was erected in the heathen temple, and on it a huge cross. Father Olmedo preached through an interpreter named Aguilar, who had been cast years before on the Yucatan coast, and the first converts from among the natives of New Spain were baptized, consisting of twenty female slaves, all of whom remained in the camp of the officers. One of these "was a young girl about eighteen years of age, of noble birth, beauty, quick genius, and great spirit." Jealousy, resulting from a second marriage, had caused her mother to cast her out, and when she grew up she was sold to the Tabascans. On being baptized she received the name of Marina, and accompanied Cortez on all his expeditions. She spoke two native languages and soon acquired the Spanish, thus making herself invaluable to the conqueror.

The Spanish fleet pushed on still in search of gold and glory. A few days later they anchored in the port of San Juan Ulua, known in modern times by the name of Vera Cruz. The brief visits of Grijalva to the Mexican coast a year prior had been communicated to the Emperor Moctezuma. Full of fear and anxiety he had determined, if possible, to prevent the coming of the "sons of Quetzalcoatl" to usurp his kingdom. He thought to do this in a diplomatic way. Hardly had the Spanish fleet entered the port when little canoes were seen putting out from shore. An embassy from the Aztec empire was reported as in waiting to extend to them a welcome. The following Sunday (Easter) Cortez was on shore, and entertained the embassy with the greatest pomp possible. He explained to them that he was the subject of Don Carlos of Austria, the greatest king of the East, whose bounty, grandeur, and power he extolled with most magnificent praises, and added that "this great monarch, knowing of that land and the lord who reigned there, sent him to make him a visit in his name, and to communicate to him in person some affairs of great importance, and that, therefore, he would be glad to know when it would please their lord to hear his embassy." *

Moctezuma's minister, not to be outdone in diplomacy, replied: "I have listened with pleasure to what you have told me concerning the grandeur and bounty of your sovereign, but know that our king is not less bountiful and great; I rather wonder that there should exist another in the world more powerful than he; but as you assert it I will make it known to my sovereign, from whose goodness I trust that he will not only have pleasure in receiving in-

* Clavigero, vol. ii, p. 280.

THE ARRIVAL OF THE SPANIARDS. 211

telligence of that great prince, but will likewise do honor to his ambassador. Accept, in the meantime, this present which I offer you in his name."

The Aztec ambassador then directed the slaves "to lay down the presents; among them were thirty bales of cotton fabrics, from gauzy curtains to heavy robes, white, colored, plain, and figured, interwoven with fantastic feathers or embroidered with gold and silver thread; humming-bird feathers and beautiful plumes of all colors, embroidered sandals, and marcasite mirrors. All these, however, were trifles beside the gold, the bright, glittering gold and the silver which were not disclosed. First there was a disk of the yellow metal, representing the sun with its rays, as large as a carriage wheel, ten spans in diameter, ornamented in semi-relief, and valued at thirty-eight hundred pesos de oro. A companion disk of solid silver, of the same size, and equally ornamented, represented the moon. Then there were thirty golden ducks, well fashioned; a number of other pieces in form of dogs, lions, monkeys, and other animals; ten collars, a necklace, with over one hundred pendant stones, called emeralds and rubies by the Spaniards; twelve arrows, a bow with cord stretched, two staves, each five palms in length; fans, bracelets, and other pieces, all of fine gold, besides a number of silver.

What could have delighted the Spaniards more? One thing only, and that was not wanting—the gilt helmet returned full of virgin gold, fine dust and coarse, with a plentiful mixture of nuggets of various sizes and shapes, all fresh from the placers. The value of these was three thousand pesos, and appreciation was attracted not so much by the amount as by the significance of the gift, as Bernal Diaz remarks, for it afforded a sure indication of the existence of rich mines in the country. Brasseur de Bourbourg estimated the gold disk alone as worth 357,380 francs, or $70,000. Doubtless, as Torquemada says, it was this gift which finally cost Moctezuma his head, for after these rich samples the hardships and dangers of the road were less than ever to Cortez. He is reported to have sent a message to Moctezuma that he and his companions had a complaint, 'a disease of the heart, which is cured by gold.'"*

This same disease afflicted him on many occasions, especially when he committed that fearful crime of burning the feet of Cuatemoctzin and his nephew, as referred to in our first lecture—a crime that will forever stain the records of the conquest. Repeated messages and additional presents from Moctezuma to Cortez and his king were only so

---

* Helps's *Life of Cortez*, vol. i, p. 56.

much fuel to the fire of the conqueror's greed. If he ever vacillated about reaching Moctezuma's capital it was not after receiving the second embassy with their precious freight of gems, various works of gold, and ten bales of most curious robes of feathers. Still later Moctezuma made another present to Cortez, of which, in July, 1519, he sent the following to Charles V :

" Two wheels ten hands in diameter, one in gold with the image of the sun, and the other of silver with the image of the moon upon it ; both formed of plates of these metals, with different figures of animals and other things in *basso-relievo*, finished with great ingenuity and art. A gold necklace, composed of seven pieces, with one hundred and eighty-three small emeralds set in it, and two hundred and thirty-two gems similar to small rubies, from which hung twenty-seven little bells of gold and some pearls. Another necklace of four pieces of gold, with one hundred and two red gems like small rubies, one hundred and seventy-two emeralds, and ten fine pearls set in, with twenty-six little bells of gold. A head-piece of wood covered with gold and adorned with gems, from which hung twenty-five little bells of gold ; instead of a plume it had a green bird with eyes, beak, and feet of gold. A bracelet of gold. A little rod like a scepter, with two rings of gold at its extremities, set with pearls. Four tridents, adorned with feathers of various colors, with pearl points tied with gold thread. Several shoes of the skin of the deer, sewed with gold thread, the soles of which were made of blue and white stone of Itztli, extremely thin. A shield of wood and leather, with little bells hanging to it and covered with plates of gold in the middle, on which was cut the image of the god of war between four heads of a lion, a tiger, an eagle, and an owl, represented alive with their hair and feathers. Several dressed skins of quadrupeds and birds with their plumage and hair. Twenty-four curious and beautiful shields of gold, of feathers and silver only. Four fishes, two ducks, and some other birds of cast gold. Two seashells of gold and a large crocodile girt with threads of gold. A large mirror adorned with gold, and many small mirrors. Several miters and crowns of feathers and gold, ornamented with pearls and gems. Several large plumes of beautiful feathers of various colors fretted with gold and small pearls. Several fans of gold and feathers mixed together; others of feathers only, of different forms and sizes, but all most rich and elegant. A variety of cotton mantles, some all white, others checkered with white and black or red, green, yellow, and blue, on the outside rough like a shaggy cloth and without color or nap.

A number of under waistcoats, handkerchiefs, counterpanes, tapestries, and carpets of cotton. All these articles were, according to Gomara, 'more valuable for the workmanship than the material. The colors,' he says, ' of the cotton were extremely fine, and those of the feathers natural. Their works of cast metal are not to be compared by our goldsmiths.'"*

This was the first gold and the first silver sent from New to Old Spain—a small presage of the immense treasures to be sent in the future, and valued at hundreds of millions in gold.

An invitation to visit Cempoala, twenty-four miles inland, was readily accepted by Cortez, especially as he hoped to make its thousands of inhabitants his allies before marching on toward the unknown and the mysterious nations hidden in the interior. Lured onward, they found Cempoala to be a beautiful city of from twenty to thirty thousand, according to Las Casas, but according to Torquemada many times larger. They were received in a most friendly way, "reveling in fruits and flowers," while a garland, chiefly of roses, was flung around the neck of Cortez, and a beautiful wreath placed upon his helmet. Chicomacatl, lord of the province, was not only cordial but communicative,

* Bancroft's *Works*, vol, ix, p. 129.

and, besides securing him fifty thousand Totonacs as friendly allies, he gave to Cortez a historic outline of the Aztecs and all the information which he so much needed. Cortez then proceeded to manifest his appreciation of all by a novel and wholesale transfer of the entire kingdom of Cempoala into the "kingdom of grace."

In the center of the beautiful city stood the temple wherein they and their fathers had worshiped for centuries. Of all it was to them the dearest and most sacred spot on earth. But Cortez determined that it must be converted into a Christian temple. So the soldiers were drawn up in a cordon around the temple, the cannon, with their concentrated thunder and lightning, were made ready, and the following grandiloquent address delivered by Cortez: "Courage, soldiers; now is the time to show that we are Spaniards, and that we have inherited from our ancestors an ardent zeal for our holy religion. Let us break the idols, and take from the sight of those unbelievers such vile incentives to their superstition."* The cacique (lord) of Cempoala made a sign to his people to prepare for the defense of their gods. But Cortez quietly informed him that if any should raise a finger against the Spaniards these would charge upon them with such

* Clavigero, vol. ii, book viii.

THE ARRIVAL OF THE SPANIARDS. 217

fury that they would not leave a native alive among them. Thereupon fifty soldiers mounted into the temple and cast every idol down the stairs, while the natives stood paralyzed. Clavigero adds : " After this daring act, where prudence was blinded by enthusiasm, Cortez commanded the priests to bring the fragments of the idols before him and throw them into a fire. He was immediately obeyed, upon which, being full of joy and triumph, as if by breaking the idols he had entirely banished idolatry and superstition from those people, he told their chief he was now willing to accept the eight virgins which had been offered him ; that from that time he would consider the Totonacs as his friends and brothers, and in all their exigencies would assist them against their enemies ; that as they could never more adore those detestable images of the demon, their enemy, he would place in the same temple an image of the true mother of God, that they might worship and implore her protection in all their necessities. He then expatiated in a long discourse upon the sanctity of the Christian religion ; after which he ordered the Cempoalese masons to cleanse the walls of the temples of those disgustful stains of human blood which they preserved there as trophies of their religion, and to polish and whiten them. He caused an altar to be made after the mode of Christians, and placed the image of the most holy Mary there." *

This was but a repetition of the conduct of the conquerors in the island of Cozumel, where, only a few weeks before, the two missionaries had vainly labored to persuade the people to destroy their idols and embrace the true faith. They failed. But, as Prescott remarks, " Cortez was probably not much of a polemic. At all events, he preferred on the present occasion action to argument, and thought the best way to convince the Indians of their error was to prove the falsehood of the prediction," † that is, that the gods would punish the proposed desecration. " He accordingly, without further ceremony, caused the venerated images to be rolled down the stairs of the great temple amid the groans and lamentations of the natives. An altar was hastily constructed, an image of the Virgin and Child placed over it, and mass was performed by Father Olmedo and his reverend companion for the first time within the walls of a temple in New Spain." ‡ The ministers tried to pour the light of their Gospel into the benighted understandings of the islanders, and to expound the mysteries of the Catholic faith. The Indian interpreter must have afforded rather

---

* Book viii. † *Conquest*, vol. i, p. 124.
‡ *Discoverers of Mexico*, Aguilar, p. 124.

THE ARRIVAL OF THE SPANIARDS. 219

a dubious channel for the transmission of such abstruse doctrines. But at length they found favor with their auditors, who, whether overawed by the bold bearing of the invaders or convinced of the impotence of deities that could not shield their own shrines from violation, consented to embrace Christianity. And this was his line of conduct throughout. Strange way was this of doing missionary work and Christianizing the natives. But such a course has left its legitimate fruits—fruits seen all over Mexico to this very day. So that the great Humboldt, visiting Mexico three hundred years later, wrote: "The introduction of the Romish religion had no other effect upon the Mexicans than to substitute ceremonies and symbols for the rites of a sanguinary worship. Dogma has not succeeded dogma, but only ceremony to ceremony. I have seen them, marked and adorned with tinkling bells, perform savage dances around the altar while a monk of St. Francis elevated the host."

Dr. Gorham D. Abbott, some years later, sums up his observations thus: "Christianity, instead of fulfilling its mission of enlightening, converting, and sanctifying the natives, was itself converted. Paganism was baptized, Christianity paganized."

The author of *Mexico in Transition* forcibly adds: " The Christianization of such a mass of humanity by a mere handful of military adventurers and their few clerical helpers, by the offhand methods which they employed, frequently at the sword's point, is an awful part of the record that has come down to us. The world never before witnessed any such process as they adopted in Christianizing those whom their cruelty spared." *

It is refreshing, indeed, to find one, if only one, among the companions of Cortez protesting against this wholesale and flimsy process of conversion. The protester was Father Las Casas, who insisted on "the futility of these forced conversions, by which it was proposed in a few days to wean men from the idolatry which they had been taught to reverence from the cradle. The only way of doing this," the good bishop said, " is by long, assiduous, and faithful preaching, until the heathen shall gather some ideas of the true nature of the Deity and of the doctrines they are to embrace. Above all, the lives of the Christians should be such as to exemplify the truth of these doctrines, that seeing this the poor Indian may glorify the Father and acknowledge him who has such worshipers for the true and only God." † He, of all others who came with the conquerors, had a right thus to talk. Such was his true apostolic spirit, such his faithful work

* Page 10.   † Quoted by Dr. Kirk in Lippincott's Prescott.

for the poor Indian, and such his upright life, that to this day his name is not only carried by one of the States of the Mexican republic, but is held in sacred remembrance by multitudes who look upon him as an exception to the ruinous rule of colonial times and tyrants.

Happy the leader who can turn the disaffection of his men to his own advantage. The excessive heat, barren coasts, annoying insects, bilious fevers, and days of idleness were enough to create dissatisfaction in the camp, and a clamor was raised favoring a speedy return to Cuba. This was no doubt fomented by personal followers of Velasquez, the lieutenant governor of the island, and of whom Cortez had reason to be apprehensive, especially in view of his (Velasquez) efforts to misrepresent him before Charles V, who had recently come to the Spanish throne. But this proved to be Cortez's hour—an hour, too, for which he had doubtless longed. Gold was coming in too rapidly, land and peoples were being conquered apace. What if all this should belong to Velasquez? When, however, the rebellion in the camp came he appeared willing to return to Cuba, and actually ordered an embarcation. But then the men were not ready to go. Hence another course was decided upon. A colony should be founded, a government should be established. This accomplished, he laid his commission upon the table before the thus "duly constituted authorities, and retired from the assembly." He was absent but a short time when, on being called in, he was informed of the fact that "they had unanimously named him, in behalf of their Catholic Highness, Captain General and Chief Justice of the Colony." He had played his part diplomatically and boldly, and henceforth was responsible for his conduct to the king and queen at Madrid, and not to their lieutenant at Cuba. From this on one fifth of all the gold and silver obtained by commerce or conquest became his personal right. Clothed with supreme civil and military jurisdiction Cortez was not backward in asserting his authority. The malcontents, even the three who had a few days before been reduced to chains, accepted the situation and, indeed, ere long became devoted partisans of Cortez. He was supreme master of the situation, at least for the time. A pompous dispatch was sent by special envoy to Spain (the original of which is preserved in the Imperial Library at Vienna), and New Spain was thus, by the fiat of one bold man, launched on the sea of nations, a sea tempestuous enough in succeeding centuries.

A second conspiracy served to make the leader bolder than ever. The two ringleaders were hung,

THE ARRIVAL OF THE SPANIARDS. 223

though it is said that Cortez, when signing their death warrants, like Nero of old, was heard to exclaim, " Would that I had never learned to write ! " Something had to be done and done quickly forever to suppress these disturbances, and Cortez secretly resolved what that something should be. They were at Cempoala, a short distance inland, so the soldiers could see and know nothing till it was all over. The something upon which he resolved was to destroy the ships and thus cut off all possibility of return to Cuba. Under the pretext that the vessels were injured by storms and also by a water insect known to be mischievously active in those tropical seas, five, and, later on, four more ships were sunk, leaving but one small vessel afloat.

After reaching this conclusion in his own mind he next sought to carry with him, if possible, the conviction of his men. Here again he was equal to the occasion. The first reports had only enraged the crowd, and they declared themselves betrayed, and being " led as lambs to the slaughter." " For shame ! be men ! " he cried. " You should know ere this how vain are the attempts to thwart my purpose. Look on this magnificent land, with its vast treasures, and narrow not your vision to your insignificant selves. Think of your glorious reward present and to come, and trust in God, who, if it so please him, can conquer this empire with a single arm. Yet, if there be one here still so craven as to wish to turn his back on the glories and advantages thus offered; if there be one here so base, so recreant to heaven, to his king, to his comrades, as to shrink from such honorable duty, in God's name let him go. There is one ship left, which I will equip at my own charge, and leave to that man the immortal infamy he deserves." *

His impassioned and nervous eloquence had the desired effect. Cortez knew his men as the good musician knows his instrument. Cheer after cheer rent the air, and when at last came a lull he quietly asked, "Would it not be well to destroy the remaining vessel and so make a safe, clean thing of it?" hearty approval was given, and again the air was rent with cries; but this time all united in exclaiming, "To Mexico! To Mexico!"

"Thus," as Robertson says, "from an effort of magnanimity, to which there is nothing parallel in history, five hundred men voluntarily consented to be shut up in a hostile country filled with powerful and unknown nations, and, having precluded any means of escape, left themselves without any resource but their own valor and perseverance." †

* Bancroft's *Works*, vol. ix, p. 184.
† *America*, p. 211.

THE ARRIVAL OF THE SPANIARDS. 225

Gibbon, in his *Decline and Fall of the Roman Empire*, cites the case of Julian, who, in his unfortunate Assyrian invasion, burnt the fleet which had carried him up the Tigris. But the historian shows that the fleet would have actually proven a hindrance rather than a help, so that we think Robertson's language cannot be regarded as extravagant when he declares Cortez's conduct " without a parallel in history."

" To success or total destruction now we march, for there is open to us no retreat!" again cried Cortez. " In Christ we trust, and on our arms rely, and, though few in numbers, our hearts are strong." *

" We are ready to obey you," came back the ready answer from hundreds of voices. " Our fortunes, for better or worse, are cast with yours." †

On the 16th of August, 1521, four hundred and fifty Spanish soldiers, with fifteen horses and six or seven light cannon, and a considerable number of friendly Indians and Cubans, with about thirteen hundred Totonacs, started up the steep Cordilleras, determined, as Cortez is reported to have said, " to tread the streets of the Mexican capital before he entered the gates of the celestial city." Following the advice of the Totonacs they chose their route through Tlaxcala, as these people were not only

* Bancroft, vol. ix, p. 191.   † Prescott, vol. i, p. 176.

friendly to the Totonacs, but ancient and deadly enemies to the Mexicans. The story of their march, their engagement with the Tlaxcalans under the valiant Xicotencatl, the subsequent declaration of peace and final alliance with these brave people, is magnificently told by the florid Prescott, the enchanting Clavigero, the prolific Bancroft, and others to whom we might refer. But we hasten to the end of the story. We pause, however, to remark that Cortez in his dispatches compared the city of Tlaxcala to Granada, saying that it was larger, stronger, and more populous than the Moorish capital at the time of the conquest.*

The little republic of Tlaxcala is said to have contained about half a million of people, one tenth of whom at least were under arms. And yet, after three battles of more or less severity, this handful of Spanish invaders were masters of the situation. It has always been a wonder that such a small number of men could have prevailed against such multitudes. There are a few simple reasons:

1. The natives were strangers to military order and discipline.

2. The imperfection of their weapons was against them. These consisted of slings, bows, and arrows, spears, sticks hardened in fire, swords of

* Clavigero, p, 323.

wood, and war clubs. Destructive enough were they among naked Indians, but most of them were of small avail against Spanish bucklers and quilted jackets.

3. The natives lost in a great measure the strength they might have derived from superior numbers by their constant solicitude to carry off the dead and wounded, even during the thick of the combat, to prevent their being devoured by the enemy.

There was a strange barbarous generosity among the natives. For instance, the Tlaxcalans advised the Spaniards of their hostile intentions, and supposing the invaders to be without provisions sent supplies of "poultry and maize" into their camp, and Herrera and Gomara further declare that "they desired them to eat plentifully, because they scorned to attack an enemy enfeebled by hunger, and it would be an affront to their gods to offer them famished victims, as well as disagreeable to feed on such emaciated prey." *

No wonder the Spaniards triumphed in Mexico. One of the most cruel deeds of the conquest was committed in Tlaxcala. Fifty spies were captured in the Spanish camp. Cortez, to show the superior power of the Christian soldiers, ordered both hands

* Quoted by Robertson, p. 214.

of the fifty Indians chopped off, and thus maimed they returned to their side of the line.

Soon after this the intrepid conqueror had the audacity to demand, with sword in hand, of the Tlaxcalans that, as a nation, they be baptized and accept Christianity. Indeed, but for the advice of Father Olmedo, he might have compelled them to do so. For Cortez certainly belonged to the Church militant, spoken of by the English poet:

> "Such as do build their faith upon
> The holy text of pike and gun,
> And prove their doctrines orthodox
> By apostolic blows and knocks."

No wonder, after all this, that as Cortez tried to insist upon the casting down of the idols and the substitution of his emblems of religion, that the Tlaxcalans replied they were willing to give the God of the Christians a place among the divinities of Tlaxcala. They were willing under threat to please their friend Cortez, especially since "their polytheistic system, like that of the ancient Greeks, was of that accommodating kind which could admit within its elastic folds the deities of any other religion without violence to itself." *

The news of Tlaxcala affairs was daily communicated to the Aztec capital, and Moctezuma's fears

* Prescott, p. 212.

were constantly on the increase. Hence he feigned to be friendly, and sent Cortez costly presents and an urgent invitation to visit him. This simply aggravated his "heart disease" and hastened his steps toward Mexico, that mysterious capital of a hitherto unconquered race.

Cholula, the holy city of Anahuac, was soon overthrown, though the massacre of six thousand men under the shadow of its gigantic pyramid makes one of the darkest pages in the annals of the conquest. A reconciliation was effected between its people and the Tlaxcalans, and Cortez's little band of foreigners headed the united forces of Cempoala, Tlaxcala, Cholula, and Huexotzinco, numbering in all some six thousand men.

The downfall of Cholula, and the silence of the Mexican gods when consulted, only served to deepen the awe of Moctezuma into terror as the Spaniards approached. The idols were again consulted and this time Huitzilopochtli suggested that the strangers be invited in, their retreat be cut off, and that they be captured and sacrificed on the altar, after which their flesh should be eaten Therefore friendly embassies with additional presents were dispatched to hasten their coming. The army continued its march, crossing the mountains between the snow-capped volcanoes of Popocatepetl and

Ixtaccihuatl, from which point the Spaniards had their first view of the magnificent valley of Mexico —a scene which Humboldt declares has few superiors in all the world. Thus between the gates of the sunset came the fair children of the sun, and the prophecy of the oldest Mexican astrologers became reality.

We must refer you to the standard histories for the narrative of the hard marches through and around the valley, the first interview with Moctezuma, the entrance into the imperial city, the long-wished-for goal, Cortez's first visit in company with the Aztec emperor to the great Teocalli, the accidental discovery of the hidden cave which fairly blazed with treasures, and the final imprisonment of Moctezuma. The subsequent events which led up to the death of Moctezuma, and the final and complete subjugation of the Aztecs to the Spaniards, consummated on the 13th of August, 1521, while of most thrilling interest, cannot here be detailed.

The conquest would, doubtless, have been an impossibility had the native tribes been united in defense of their common country. Be that as it may, we have the wonderful spectacle presented to the world of a few hundred Europeans, with their superior arms, and doubtless aided by the divisions and the superstitions of the natives, becoming masters of

THE ARRIVAL OF THE SPANIARDS. 231

many millions of Mexicans. And of these millions they became the earthly masters for three hundred years. Well may the world ask, With what results?

The chief centers of population were finally led to an outward acceptance of the forms and ceremonies of Christianity. The rural and mountain districts, too often like the Tlaxcalans, were willing to place the God of the Christians among their other deities, and to this day their religious feasts justify the opinion of Humboldt, already quoted, concerning the mixture of savage and Christian ceremonies. To the world it was announced that a nation had been Christianized. But among the members of the Church making this empty boast are found to-day, as well as in the past, wise men who do not hesitate, like Abbé Emanuel Domenech, to assert that "the Mexican faith is a dead faith," and "the Mexican is not a Catholic; he is simply a Christian, because he has been baptized." *

What Spain did for Mexico in this and other senses is so well told by one of Mexico's noblest and most eloquent sons, that we quote at length from a speech which the Hon. Ignacio Ramirez made a few years since before one of the lyceums of the city of Mexico. We have two objects in making the lengthy quotation; one is to give a

* *Mexico and the United States*, Abbott, pp. 195-203.

sample of native eloquence (for Judge Ramirez was a pure Indian), and the other is to show how intelligent Mexicans of the present age regard the people by whom they were conquered three hundred and fifty years ago. This learned but now lamented Indian said:

"The ephemeral grandeur of Spain overawes the mind. Southern nations were accustomed, in times of peace, to ornament their conquerors' weapons with emeralds and diamonds; but the Spaniards, after two thousand years of conflict, from the times of the Carthaginians to the capture of Granada, became so unnatural that, even when the world was at their feet, they found no time to cleanse the escutcheon of the Cid or of Pelayo. They did not enjoy opulence for a single day. They rendered homage to a foreigner, and the latter dedicated the fabulous heritage of the Catholic kings to the most daring schemes. On the death of Charles V Spain found her people scattered by long distances, her agriculture harvested by the Moors, her industries victimized, her commerce discounted, her wise men burned as heretics, her municipal liberties circumscribed by prison bars, her fleets in the hands of pirates, and her only recompense Philip II, the Inquisition, and the Jesuits. Her great captains, her skilled diplomats, her profound savants, in

THE ARRIVAL OF THE SPANIARDS. 233

Flanders in France, in Italy, in the Lepant Seas, arose to the occasion in Europe, forgetting that their luminous glory and their skill might properly lay broad the foundations of future nationalities on the golden soil of the New World. Mexico was not entered, at first, save by miserable adventurers, commercial pirates, knights of the sword and incest.

"Columbus, following doubtful tracks, died in the belief that the Antilles formed part of the East Indies, and that he had discovered the gates of paradise and caught glimpses of its heavenly foliage. Cortez assassinated kings without daring to usurp their thrones, and, vested with the title of a marquis, posed before the courts of Europe as an ennobled lackey. The Spanish 'Audience' was converted into a market place, where the Indian and his wealth were placed at public auction. The wise men denied to the Aztecs even the gift of reason. The sailors were unable to make a chart of the seas they overran, and, against the protest of wiser heads, regarded Yucatan and Lower California as islands. The historians authorized the most absurd fables. The bishops prepared the miracles and apparitions which one century later were to be consecrated as authentic. The Portuguese merchants themselves saw their goods confiscated, and were likewise burned at the stake as usurers. Laws were concocted, and then put into play whereby Mexico should not produce wines, nor silks, nor pottery, nor tobacco, but should simply supply to the conquerors the precious metals. The shops and the seas were closed; the colleges were hidden in the convents, with an inquisitor as the jailer. The Jesuits conspired against the Franciscans, the Dominicans and Augustines, sole protectors of the Indians. The protection imparted to the Indians was limited to a declaration that they were simply minors.

"With the viceregal government appeared a constant order of things, the sanction of all the monstrosities of the conquest. No one in the list of viceroys and archbishops was elevated enough to keep pace with the contemporaneous events of Europe. The nobles of Mexico saw in reform a scandal; in the commercial battles of Holland and England a nursery for filibusters; in French philosophy an eternal anathema; in the emancipation of the United States a menace; in the expulsion of the Jesuits a state secret; in the relations with China a market of fans and combs; in the colonial government a mere speculation; in the middle classes burden bearers, and in the Indian but an animal. Three kinds of slavery, with these elements, were firmly established in New Spain, each a distinct system

THE ARRIVAL OF THE SPANIARDS. 235

of tyranny, to wit, the king, the pope, and foreign commercial control.

" During the colonial times the Indian policy was reduced to the sustenance of a viceroy easily replaced, under the keen eye of a scrutinizing 'Audience.' This body had judicial jurisdiction and police jurisdiction over the colonies. Spain only recognized America in as far as the latter contributed to her revenues. It mattered not in Spain whether the Indians were rational beings or mere brutes, freemen or slaves, or whether they were preserved or annihilated. At times Spain became alarmed, for the rich soil of Mexico produced what easily competed with the products of Europe. She scorned our advances in civilization, and was only pleased when the vessels laden with gold and silver reached the wharves of Cadiz. She deigned likewise to accept as gifts either an idol or a cacique (native chieftain).

" The clergy with rare discretion never lost an opportunity for extending and strengthening their own influence. For three hundred years the clergy governed Mexico by means of bishops and archbishops, seated on the thrones of the viceroys. They even held the lay viceroys themselves in their power, under the threat of excommunication. The clergy served as friendly arbiters among the peoples recently converted; they legislated in their very missions; they monopolized public education; they became capitalists, and in their acts of usury far surpassed the Shylocks of the Middle Ages. The Jesuits were their secret police and the Inquisition was a living tomb. They mingled their European blood with that of the Indian, and then conferred on their bastard offspring the Church's best curates. They raised cathedrals of mocking splendor and built great convents and churchly retreats, while the viceroys built jails, mints, and tax offices. They fixed civil time to the exigencies of numerous feasts and religious practices. They mingled the Indian and the Spaniard in one flock, and merged God and the pope into two invisible sovereignties. Madrid was for us but an office of Rome.

"Another power meanwhile grew rapidly and became a menace to the Spaniards, to the clergy themselves, and to the indigenous classes. Foreign commerce, piratical, authorized in its contraband features, under contract and without, flooded with their effects all of desolated Spain and its idle colonies. . . . The nations directly interested in free commerce were France, England, and the United States. Spain, exorcised in Charles II the Bewitched, had at the head of affairs Fernando VII, while its emblem was the green candle of the Inquisition, its assistants were resurrected Jesuits, and its exchequer was debt. Mexico, in such conditions, should be civilly emancipated from the clergy; but another struggle had to ensue ere the chains placed by priestly hands could break.

"The administrative chaos, called the colonial *régime*, presented various phenomena. Some classes were born and others died. Can the loss ever be realized to the native races worn away on the wheel of events in Tenochtitlan? For three hundred years two hundred thousand men, half of them of the Tlaltelolco race, occupied this famous capital. Where are they now? If we glance over Lower California, there in Todos Santos, we might find perhaps one old Indian, bowed and blind, bent under the weight of fourscore years, and he even perhaps now sleeps with his fathers. It only needed six or seven Jesuits to depopulate that Californian peninsula. On the other hand, the preponderant Mexican race feels coursing through its veins the mercurial blood of every nation in the world. Religion and despotism have engendered equality.

"Unfortunately idleness characterized life in the colonies. The civil and the religious authorities worked but an hour or two during half the days of the year. The owners of plantations trusted their properties to the foreman or the lessee, while many were parasites by profession. Foreign nations have surprised us with our coasts deserted, our country without roads, our people uninspired by the arts or dead to great business ventures; absolutely ignorant of our own wonderful resources, and only able to acquire the envied possessions of another people when our miners sent abroad our precious metals. Spain lost her colonies because she only cherished therein tax collectors, priests and miners."*

The educated Indian, now constantly growing in numbers, in our sister republic, will never have this awful picture erased from his mind. No wonder that, as he reflected how all this was done in the name of the holy Catholic faith, he often asked, "Where is God?" While some of the more religiously inclined were led to cry out, "How long, O Lord, how long!"

*Obras de Ignacio Ramirez, pp. 230–235.

LECTURE VII.

INDEPENDENCE AND THE CONSTITUTION OF 1857.

LECTURE VII.

INDEPENDENCE AND THE CONSTITUTION OF 1857.

THE sentiments so eloquently expressed by the lamented Ramirez were entertained by at least three fourths of the inhabitants of the country in the early part of this century. The perpetual drainage of the country's wealth by means of all kinds of taxation, the practical inthralldom of the indigenous races, their " lack of knowledge and no means placed within their reach to secure it," proved too conclusively to the poor Mexican that the Spaniards never recovered from the dreadful " disease of the heart which gold alone could cure," announced by Cortez, and that this disease, so frequently manifested during the conquest and the colonial times, was in no way lessening. They, the lawful owners of the country, became but the unfortunate victims of intruders. They could only judge by results. They had been conquered in the name of the King of Spain and the holy father in Rome. The former, in robbing them of their country, had cruelly burned the feet of two of their native rulers to compel them to reveal their hidden treasures—a cruelty kept up, in a modified sense, through all the three centuries; while the representatives of the latter, from the time of Bishop Zumarraga down to the ecclesiastics of the nineteenth century, not only shared this "cursed lust of gold" with the civil oppressors, but had, as a rule, done comparatively little to educate or elevate the Mexicans. Indeed, since the day in 1530 that Zumarraga had collected all their beautiful works of art—"their abominable scrolls and manuscripts, wherein every sign or picture seemed to the prelate the embodiment of Satanic art and witchery"—gathered them from public places and private homes, and cast them into one vast pile in the market place to be burned, the representatives of the Church showed clearly the fear entertained by them that the world at large might learn something of the civilization which they were despoiling in Mexico. Not only the civilization and arts of the natives, but their families as well were despoiled by priest and soldier. Immediately following the triumph of Cortez, when the Mexican prince warned him that if their "wives and daughters were not returned to their homes there might be a revolt among the Indians," and down to modern times, both Spanish priest and ruler have constantly invaded households and dragged souls into "the gall of bitterness." In early colonial times concubinage among the priests was only punished when it became too public and too scandalous.

So at last when they realized the burden of centuries—" iron despotism, in which priest and soldier bore an equal part "—and aspirations after independence and liberty had been burning in their secret souls for many a long day, the " Grito de Dolores," raised in 1810 by the venerable curate, Hidalgo, found ready response in every corner of the land, and with reason, too. From 1535 to 1821 sixty-one foreign viceroys had governed Mexico. Domineering in the exercise of their absolute rule, and in the monopoly of places of trust and power, they oppressed and insulted the natives till intense hatred of everything Spanish became the natural result. Even the Creole descendants were by law prohibited from participation in government service.

Legislation in Madrid concerning New Spain was exclusive and oppressive, so much so that certain industries, such as the raising of silkworms and the cultivation of the vine, to which the climate and soil of Mexico were, and are now, peculiarly adapted, were interdicted—thus compelling Mexico to buy of Spain. The owners of many of the largest estates lived across the Atlantic and drew their revenues out of the country. Others lived in the capital, who seldom if ever saw their great farms, which were managed, as in the former case, by administradores. In 1803 José de Iturrigaray came from Spain as viceroy. But his inclination to give the Creoles a chance cost him his position. Being hastily removed, the archbishop was placed in power till the arrival of a new viceroy, a more reliable Tory.

"The French Revolution and the changes made by the movements of Napoleon I, including the removal of the Bourbon from the throne of Spain, reduced the prestige of Spanish rule in Mexico and seriously lessened the power of the viceroys. This was intensified when the emperor placed his brother on the Spanish throne, thus giving a heavy shock to the doctrine of the 'divine right of kings' and the immutability of established order, and raising hopes that changes in the interests of liberty and right were to be expected and welcomed, and, if need be, fought for, by those who appreciated the sentiment, 'Who would be free himself must strike the blow.' The spirit of liberty became infectious, and was strengthened by the Constitution granted by the new Cortes of Spain in 1812, which abolished the Inquisition and gave to Mexico more freedom than she had known since the conquest. But the viceroy was a true absolutist, and had no heart to welcome the beneficent change, and longed for its overthrow. The fall of Napoleon was followed by the removal of his brother and the change of the liberal regimen in Spain. Ferdinand VII, who was restored to the throne by the policy of the 'allied powers,' who met in Paris to reconstruct the map of Europe, was one of the most despotic of the Bourbons.

"He abolished the Constitution, restored the Inquisition and absolute government, and once more oppressed the inhabitants of the Spanish peninsula. Stern orders were sent to withdraw all that had been conceded to the people of Mexico.

"Fearing the progress of the liberal ideas in that country as well as in the South American colonies, Ferdinand was intending to dispatch a fleet and army to bring Mexico and South American colonies again into submission. Before it was ready to sail the discovery was made that many of the officers had become infected with this 'new fever of liberty,' and even dared to express their displeasure at the service demanded of them, and were, indeed, more likely to lead the revolt in Mexico than to suppress it. None others could take their places, and Ferdinand and his clerical sympathizers were openly criticised for their despotic plans till, alarmed for the stability of his throne, the Constitution was restored and the hostile expedition to Mexico abandoned." *

The cradle of Mexican independence was the central State of Guanajuato. Here the leaven of liberty had been working for some time in a little town called Dolores, about twenty-five miles from the State capital, and a great mining center. The curate of this town was Miguel Hidalgo y Costilla, a name worthy of lasting honor as of one who gave his life to his country and "who sacrified himself for the right as against injustice and oppression." He had already reached the age—about sixty—when most men seek rest from life's burdens. And yet he voluntarily placed his shoulders under the burdens of a nation while many thought the time not yet ripe.

This "Washington" of his country is described by Bancroft as follows: "His heart was kind and sympathetic; his manner soft and winning; his voice sonorous, vibrating, and most pleasing to the ear, and his deportment was natural and attractive. He had the true scholarly stoop, and in all his features, air, and attitude a profoundly meditative expression—a fitting incarnation of a great soul bathed in settled calm. Yet the clear, black, brilliant eyes

* *Mexico in Transition*, William Butler, D. D., p. 65.

betrayed the activity of the mind, and through them shone the light from the burning fires within." *

This kind and sympathetic curate, like a father to his flock, was interested in everything related to their temporal and spiritual welfare. So he taught them, among other things, grape culture and to raise silkworms, and he also built a porcelain factory. But these innocent occupations, likely to improve their temporal condition, thought at the time to cut off so much revenue from the home government, proved too much for the viceroy. So special agents were dispatched speedily to Dolores, and the worthy curate stood helplessly by while every mulberry tree was cut down and every vine torn up. Hidalgo had been for some time in secret correspondence with Allende, Aldama, and other patriots in the city of Querétaro, under the guise of a literary academy, where they were greatly helped by one Miguel Dominguez and his estimable wife, Doña Josefa Maria Ortiz. To this intelligent and patriotic woman was due the success of many early movements when the cause seemed weak. Noble women in State and Church have often lent inspiration and direction to worthy causes in trying hours.

The cruel destruction of his industry thoroughly

* Bancroft's *Works*, vol. xii, p. 104.

aroused the curate and his neighbors for many miles around. Indeed, the indignation spread far and wide, like the echo from the Boston Tea Party of 1776. The members of the Literary Academy in Querétaro, and other sympathizers throughout the land, concluded that the time to strike had come. On the night of the 15th of September, of the year already referred to, Hidalgo, in the public square of Dolores, raised his Grito, " Viva la Independencia, Muera el Gobierno." This was afterward changed to " Mueran los Gachupines," * and a few days later at Atotonilco were added the words, " Viva la Virgen de Guadalupe."†

The workmen in Hidalgo's two factories were forewarned and soon appeared with arms in hand. The nineteen Spanish residents of the town were put under arrest. As dawn approached the church bell was rung that Sunday morning at an earlier hour than usual, the first tolling of Mexico's liberty bell. The townspeople gathered, and at a late hour the people flocked in from the neighboring farms. The faithful pastor of many years had a new and novel text, " Deliverance was demanded, and from the evil one; but it was from Satan in the flesh, from devils incarnate as temporal masters, inflicting

---

* A contemptuous name for the Spaniards.
‡ *Mexico Á Traves de los Siglos*, vol. iii. p 107.

wrongs and injuries and infamies without number."* As the curate entered the pulpit and looked on the sea of upturned anxious faces he said, "My dear children, this day comes to us a new dispensation. Are you ready to receive it? Will you be free? Will you make the effort to recover from the hated Spaniards the lands stolen from your forefathers three hundred years ago?"

This was the first public speech of the Revolution, and it was the last made by this pastor to his flock at Dolores. Like loving children, terribly in earnest, they followed their spiritual guide and their patriotic leader out of town that morning, about six hundred strong. Lances, machetes, clubs, slings, bows, and arrows, were their chief weapons—of firearms they had but few. At San Miguel Allende their number rose to four thousand, and a supply of munitions of war was secured. On the 18th, just two days after the "Grito," as they marched out of San Miguel the forces numbered ten thousand; on the 21st they reached Querétaro, and a few days later entered Celaya with an army of fifty thousand. Here Hidalgo was elected captain general amid the wild enthusiasm of his followers. On the morning of the 28th they approached the city of Guanajuato, were joined by a considerable army of miners, and

* Bancroft's *Works*, vol. xii, p. 117.

after four hours' struggle they took the city. With it fell into their hands additional munitions of war and about one million dollars found in the State treasury. Soon after Valladolid, Guadalajara, and other cities were in their possession. The wonderful success attending Hidalgo's movements threw consternation into the government camp at the national capital. The viceroy, knowing the power of money, offered ten thousand dollars for the body of Hidalgo "dead or alive." Anathemas and excommunications were hurled by the archbishop against Hidalgo and his associates, and, thinking to cap the climax, the rector of the university publicly announced the fact that " Hidalgo was not a doctor of divinity."

Notwithstanding all this Hidalgo turned his face toward Mexico city, evidently disposed to "beard the lion in his den." His forces constantly grew in number till, when he reached Las Cruces, a high eminence overlooking the beautiful valley of Mexico, there were nearly one hundred thousand men, women, and children following his little banner. At his feet lay the national capital, all important to him and to his cause. But, looking around him, he saw an immense rabble without discipline and without the necessary munitions of war, while the capital was defended by a royal garrison with the best armaments of the times and well-disciplined men. Hidalgo realized it was more the part of prudence to defer the attack till he was better prepared. So he turned his army northward and intended to push on toward our frontier in the hope of purchasing arms and ammunition, and at the same time drill his raw army. He was soon overtaken by the Royalists, who seriously damaged his forces, although most of them kept together till they reached Saltillo early in 1811. Here he left General Rayon in charge while, with a small escort, he pushed on toward Texas in search of the much-needed military equipment, and possibly in the hope of securing aid from the new and patriotic republic north of the Rio Grande.

About this time Hidalgo received a letter from the viceroy offering pardon in case he and his would lay down their arms. To this he replied: "We will not lay aside our arms until we have wrested the jewel of liberty from the hands of the oppressor. . . . Pardon, your excellency, is for criminals, not for defenders of their country."

A few days later this noble patriot was betrayed by a miserable traitor named Elizondo, who handed him over to the Spaniards. After being kept in prison for three months he was tried by an ecclesiastical court. On July 29 he was degraded from the priesthood, handed over to the secular court, and on the morning of the 31st was shot, his companions in arms, Allende, Aldama, and Jimenez, having been shot a few days before. The heads of all four were placed on long poles and elevated on the corners of the Alhondiga en Guanajuato, and their bodies interred in the Chapel of San Francisco. After the triumph of the revolution in 1823 an appreciative national congress ordered the bodies and the skulls removed and reinterred with solemn honors beneath the "Altar of the Three Kings," under the dome of the cathedral in the capital. Well does the author of *Mexico in Transition* remark that:

"Certainly Hidalgo could not have dreamed of the glorious part which his tattered flag should bear in the future. Year by year, on the eve of September 16, the highest national holiday, at 11 o'clock P. M., in the Hall of Representatives, the president, his cabinet, and the members of Congress, public men of Mexico, with all the brilliancy of society in the capital, crowd the structure and wait for the moment when the hands of the clock reach the hour at which Hidalgo first raised the cry of independence. Then the President of Mexico raises the old flag, waves it three times, and repeats the Grito: 'Viva la Libertad! Viva la Republica!

Viva Mexico!' and the great audience rises to join in the shout, 'Viva la Republica!' as if they would lift the roof off the building. The thunder of the artillery gives its response to the popular joy, and more than three thousand people in the capital, and, indeed, the whole nation, remember gratefully the man who died to make them free." *

His fellow-countrymen have gratefully embalmed his memory, "and his name, growing brighter and brighter as the ages pass, will be handed down unsullied to remotest generations." †

The leader was dead, but not the cause. Martyrs never help the opposite side. After Hidalgo's death the command devolved upon Morelos and Rayon. The former, an old friend and student of Hidalgo, soon became immensely popular, and came to be known as "the hero of a hundred battles." The army recovered speedily from the fall of its former leaders, and increased in numbers and multiplied its victories. From the Royalists whole companies and regiments passed over to the standard of the Republicans. The Bravos, Victoria, Bustamante, Guerrero, and others soon joined the patriot ranks.

In October, 1814, a Constitution was proclaimed,

* *Mexico in Transition*, p. 10.
† Bancroft, vol. xii, p. 286.

having been prepared by a congress called for the purpose by Morelos, and which met in Chilpancingo. The custody of this national body cost the general his life. The viceroy ordered that "the insurgents should be pursued, incarcerated, and killed like wild beasts." The Republicans, on the contrary, acted with magnanimity toward their ememy. Let the following serve as an illustration: In the ranks of the Republicans were two generals named Bravo— father and son. The father was taken a prisoner at Cauatla, tried, and condemned to die. The viceroy, knowing his value as a soldier, offered him his life if he would induce his son and his brothers to join the Royalists, but this offer was spurned. He preferred to die for his country than to live with its oppressors. While he was a prisoner the junior Bravo captured three hundred Spanish soldiers and offered them to the viceroy as a ransom for his father. Some of them were officers from Spain, and others wealthy hacendados; but the viceroy rejected the offer and ordered the father executed.

On hearing this the son was overwhelmed with grief, and he immediately ordered his three hundred prisoners shot. They were allowed religious counsel and told to prepare for execution on the following morning. On reflection, however, he concluded that their execution would be a dishonor to the cause of independence, however the world might justify it on military grounds, so he determined on his course. The next morning early the three hundred men were drawn up in line in front of the army, all ready for the fatal order. When the time for giving the order arrived Bravo rode out to the front and thus addressed the condemned men:

"Your lives are forfeited. Your master, Spain's minion, has murdered my father, murdered him in cold blood for choosing Mexico and liberty before Spain and her tyrannies. Some of you are fathers, and may imagine what my father felt in being thrust from the world without one farewell word from his son; aye, and your sons may feel a portion of that anguish of soul which fills my heart as thoughts arise of my father's wrongs and cruel death. And what a master is this of yours! For one life, my poor father's, he might have saved you all, and would not! So deadly is his hate that he would sacrifice three hundred of his friends rather than forego this one sweet morsel of vengeance. Even I, who am no viceroy, have three hundred lives for my father's. But there is a nobler revenge than this. Go! You are all free! Go find your vile master, and henceforth serve him if you can!"

No wonder it is said that "the effect was overwhelming." The entire number, "with tears streaming from their eyes rushed forward and offered their services to his cause, and remained faithful to him and to it to the very end."

It is doubtful if the difficulties and perplexities of the situation in Mexico at this time have ever been fully appreciated in the United States. In the struggle for independence theirs was a much greater task than ours. "When our patriot fathers here pledged 'life and fortune and sacred honor,' to become independent and free, they had not been for three hundred years crushed down in ignorance and poverty, almost without hope or aspiration. No powerful viceroy wielding the military forces of a foreign despot was in power to repress every utterance for liberty, or 'to hunt them down like beasts of prey' when they attempted to obtain it. No great landed aristocracy, owning every acre of the soil, laid its heavy hand upon them in vengeance. No wealthy established Church united its ghostly power with civil despotism to repress them, bringing to its aid the remorseless Inquisition and its spiritual maledictions, adding blasphemously the terrors of God and of eternity to crush their cause and their hopes as unlawful. Nor were they cut off from the sea and its resources, or left without one friendly nation on the earth to extend sympathy or a helping hand to them in the unequal struggle,

Independence and the Constitution. 257

nor so destitute of resources that they had to win battles to obtain weapons and ammunition to continue the conflict. All that they had to begin with were their own right hands and noble leaders, who 'loved not their lives unto the death,' to make their nation a land of liberty." *

Besides, in all their territory there was no common school, no elementary literature, and no Bible. Doubtful indeed it is if any people ever won constitutional liberty against greater odds. But the United States set them the example twenty-five years before, and our admiration for their persistent and brave effort cannot be too great. Had there been no historic Washington there would have been no historic Hidalgo.

After the events now described the revolution spread until the entire country was one great field of commotion, no great battle anywhere, but local uprisings on every hand.

In 1820, when it was thought by some that possibly Ferdinand VII, now restored to Spain, due to the disturbances in Europe, might seek a more quiet throne in Mexico, many liberals were led, by the hope of obtaining constitutional liberty, to consent to a temporary cessation of hostilities, especially as the home government saw fit to remove the despotic

* *Mexico in Transition.*

viceroy and put in his place a more considerate one. Iturbide, commander of the Royalist army in the southwest, issued the Plan of Iguala, or the Constitution of the Three Guarantees—religion, independence, and union. Roman Catholicism was to be the national religion, to the exclusion of all others; independence from Spain was to be had; and a union, with equal rights for all classes of people. The masses at first regarded it with favor, but the more intelligent leaders concluded that it smacked too much of Rome. The new viceroy and Iturbide met in August of that year and discussed the situation, and the former accepted with few modifications, the Plan of Iguala, agreeing himself to become a member of the Provisional Junta till Ferdinand should arrive. But Ferdinand decided not to come, as did also the crown princes of Spain, and the whole plan failed. The viceroy died suddenly, and the ambitious Iturbide was virtually master of the situation. The first article of his plan declared, "The Mexican nation is independent of the Spanish nation, and of every other, even on its own continent."

Spain was too much engaged with internal and continental disturbances at home to make more than a formal protest. But no more blood was shed, and on February 24, 1821, the Spanish flag which had floated for just three hundred years in the balmy air of New Spain was hauled down, the Mexican tricolor floated over the liberated land, and the United States of Mexico began their independent national life, the legitimate result of the life and sacrifices of Miguel Hidalgo; a result that cost the nation thousands of lives and rivers of blood.

Iturbide and Guerrero had joined forces to bring about the final result; and had the former been more of a patriot and less of a churchman he might have been elected president of the new republic. His ambition, however, was not for his country, but for himself; and when, on May 22, 1822, by the aid of the yet dominant Church party, he managed to have himself proclaimed Augustine I, Emperor of Mexico, he did not realize that by that act he had lost his hold on the best people of the nation. This, however, he soon after did realize, and then tendered his resignation. His resignation was not accepted, but he was exiled and promised to live abroad. Attempting to return about fourteen months later, he was arrested on landing and executed. His only son went to the United States for his education, and then married. To him was born one son, who to this day is spoken of by the Church party as Prince Augustine, but whose every move is watched by the liberal party.

About this time Santa Ana first prominently appeared on the scene by pronouncing against Iturbide. Some Republican leaders, believing Santa Ana to be honest in his liberal professions, joined him. After the fall of Iturbide's empire General Victoria was chosen president, and a Constitution adopted modeled after ours, save in the one proviso of religious liberty.

Spain's spasmodic and futile efforts in 1829 to regain possession of Mexico, by sending General Barrandas with a small army, only intensified native hatred toward all Spaniards, and came near resulting in their complete exile from the country.

Perhaps no public man did more to postpone Mexico's complete freedom than did Antonio Lopez de Santa Ana. His own people never knew where to find him, yet "his clerical patrons knew well how to utilize his remarkable qualities, though it must be confessed that his eye to the main chance was always as keenly open for his own advantage as for the promotion of their purposes." He was ruler of his country on five different occasions, and helped to depose about a score from the same high position. His relations to Texas gave Americans an opportunity to hear much—and especially much that was bad—about this notorious character. Perhaps no one's opinion of Santa

INDEPENDENCE AND THE CONSTITUTION. 261

Ana was as elevated as his own, for to himself he was a great hero. When he was captured by General Houston he had the audacity to remark to the general, "You are born to no common destiny who are the conqueror of the 'Napoleon of the South.'" As far back as we can remember in early school days we recall pictures of this remarkable man in our text-books, and then can remember vividly how twenty years ago this coming summer we sat by his side in the city of Mexico and heard from the lips of the feeble old man some of the events of his checkered and stormy life.

A most interesting account of the strange and pompous burial of his "Christian leg," shot off by a French cannon ball, of his assumption of dictatorial powers, his rupture with the archbishop, the desertion of his own followers, the mob that disinterred his poor leg and kicked it through the streets of the city, and the subsequent events of a career without parallel, together with an excellent portrait of the turbulent dictator, may be found in Dr. William Butler's *Mexico in Transition*.

Santa Ana's expedition to Texas was a failure, and the "Lone Star" asked for admission to the United States after ten years of independence. The final result was one of the most unrighteous wars ever waged. A war it was against which some of our best statesmen protested, and which was condemned in unqualified terms by the voice and pen of our lamented General Grant. In his *Memoirs* he says:

"The presence of the United States troops on the edge of the disputed territory farthest from the Mexican settlements was not sufficient to provoke hostilities. We were sent to provoke a fight, but it was essential that Mexico should commence it. It was very doubtful whether Congress would declare war, but if Mexico should attack our troops the executive could announce, 'Whereas, war exists by the acts of,' etc., and prosecute the contest with vigor" (Vol. i, p. 67).

"The occupation, separation, and annexation were, from the inception of the movement to its final consummation, a conspiracy to acquire territory out of which slave States might be formed for the American Union. Even if the annexation itself could be justified the manner in which the subsequent war was forced upon Mexico cannot. The fact is, annexationists wanted more territory than they could possibly lay any claim to as part of the new acquisition. Texas, as an independent State, never had exercised jurisdiction over the territory between the Nueces River and the Rio Grande. Mexico had never recognized the independence of

Texas, and maintained that, even if independent, the State had no claim south of the Nueces" (Vol. i, p. 54).

The Southern representatives in our national Congress hoped thus to secure a territory out of which nine slave States could be carved equal in extent to the State of Kentucky, as said Senator Benton, of Missouri, in his famous speech, while Mr. Wise, of Virginia, added : " Slavery should pour itself abroad without restraint, and find no limit but the Southern ocean."*

Great Britain had in 1829 offered $5,000,000 simply to take Texas under her protection. Our minister at Mexico, Mr. Poinsett, offered a like sum or a loan of $10,000,000. Mr. William Jay, in his *Review of the Causes and Consequences of the Mexican War* (Boston, 1849), shows conclusively, we think, how the government at Washington from this time forward pursued precisely the policy that provoked Mexico to declare war. Such a course with a weaker neighbor, and with the nefarious purpose of acquiring more territory, in order that the awful crime of human slavery might be perpetuated on the American continent, was a crime perhaps without equal in the history of any Christian nation. The calamity which followed a few years later in con-

* Jay's *Review*, p. 80.

nection with the same inhuman question would seem like a just dispensation from "the God of all the earth," who could look with "no degree of allowance" upon such a wicked institution as slavery. Nor should it be forgotten that Mexico, having herself abolished slavery in 1829, at the instance of the immortal Hidalgo, protested against the desecration of Texan territory by Southern slaveholders.

The largest map of the United States known to exist is not found in our colleges, but it hangs in the library of the Propaganda in Rome. On it the pope has marked, for many long years past, the march of civilization on our peerless Western continent. It is said that every town or village in our country is constantly in evidence before this keen student of geography and history. In the early forties California, no doubt, was a study of unusual interest to the pope and the Propaganda. Great Britain was also interested, as naturally were the United States. A race was made for the prize. Dr. Ellinwood, Secretary of the Presbyterian Board of Missions, in an article published in the *New York Evangelist* (June 30, 1887), tells how one Father McNamara, an Irish Romanist in California, wrote a letter to the President of Mexico asking for a concession to plant in the beautiful valley of San Joa-

INDEPENDENCE AND THE CONSTITUTION. 265

quin a colony of Irish Catholics. His letter, which was intercepted, reads as follows:

"I have a triple object in my proposal. I wish, first, to advance the cause of Catholicism; second, to promote the happiness and thrift of my countrymen; and, thirdly, to put an obstacle in the way of the further usurpations of that irreligious and anti-Catholic nation, the United States. And if the plan which I propose be not speedily adopted, your excellency may be assured that before another year the Californians will form a part of the American nation, the Catholic institutions will become the prey of the Methodist wolves, and the whole country will be inundated with cruel invaders."

We might remark, parenthetically, that the "Methodist wolves" did get there, and that one of the honored founders of Syracuse University, Jesse T. Peck, was of the first to arrive, and a very good specimen he was of the flock which has been pouring in ever since. Records in the State Department at Washington confirm the truth of the McNamara incident. True, the McNamara grant of land was made, but the British Admiral Seymour arrived too late to back the claim, and on the very day the grant was made General Fremont ran up the Stars and Stripes at Monterey, and thus secured the great gold State to the American Union. One year later

(February 2, 1848) the treaty of Guadalupe-Hidalgo closed the Mexican War, and our government paid $18,250,000 for California, a tithe, however, of what it was worth.

Two occurrences during the Mexican War should have special mention. On these two occasions, at least, at Monterey and Cherubusco, Irish soldiers in the American army, when brought face to face with the enemy, deserted the Stars and Stripes and passed over into the ranks of the Mexicans rather than fight against Roman Catholics. They were Irish emigrants who had gone into the war for pay— who received month after month the American dollar, but when the emergency came, at the mandate of a Catholic priest, they turned their backs on the flag they had sworn to defend. Let Americans remember this is what Rome may do for them in an emergency. At Cherubusco, the second place named, nearly two hundred such Irish Catholics deserted and then turned their bayonets on their fellow-countrymen. Their treachery aided the enemy in entailing upon our forces its greatest loss during the entire war, namely, one thousand killed and wounded, one seventh of the entire force. This reminds us of the startling fact recently published by Dr. R. S. MacArthur, of New York city, that, during our late rebellion seventy-two per cent of all desertions from the Union army were Irishmen, and that these desertions began just after the pope recognized the Confederacy.*

Let Americans remember that in the defense of their republican liberties neither nihilists, anarchists, revolutionary socialists, nor Roman Catholics can be fully depended upon. The latter will obey their priests quicker than their conscience or their civil ruler, for they are Romanists first and Americans after. It is a thought which may well give us some concern, with these facts before us, that all over this fair land, living under the protection of its laws, enjoying every immunity common to our people, are thousands of men who would this very day lay down their lives to obey the orders which come to them from the Tiber rather than those which come to them from the capital on the Potomac ; and who can tell but that Satolli is now instructing them how to do it? "Put none but Americans on guard to-night" may be as necessary a precaution in days to come as it has been in days that are passed.

It must be remembered that Mexico was a land without the Bible and without the common school. However unrighteous may have been the action of our government in waging war with our next-door neighbors, God always knows how to make even

* *New York Tribune*, quoted in *Pittsburg Advocate*.

the mistakes, as well as "the wrath of man to praise him." When our army marched from the Rio Grande to the interior of the country colporteurs of the American Bible and American Tract Societies followed everywhere in their wake, and under the protection of the Stars and Stripes hundreds of copies of the word of God and thousands of little tracts bearing the promise of salvation were scattered everywhere, like white-winged messengers of peace. A few of the priests and hundreds of the people received them gladly. As soon as the war was over many of these Bibles and tracts were gathered up and destroyed by order of the Church. But enough of them remained to be considered the first "seed sowing" of the glorious harvest now being gathered. Missionaries now moving about the country frequently find little groups who had secretly guarded the sacred treasure till the Bible burners ceased to have the upper hand in the country, and they were able to bring forth the Scriptures for the light and joy of little circles which, in many cases, rapidly developed into evangelical churches. On one occasion, when traveling in the hot country, and passing through a cornfield, we were arrested by the voice of song. Following the sound of a familiar tune for a short distance, we soon found ourselves in front of a little adobe hut, where sat, in the doorway, an aged Mexican and a child on either side of him. A large book lay open on his lap and a small one in his hand. To the children he was teaching what proved to be one of our Gospel hymns, and, upon inquiring, we were told that the large book was a copy of the Holy Scriptures which had been left by "a man who came with the American army in 1847." Learning we were friends, the poor Indian received us with joy, and seemed as much delighted as ourselves as we were shown the little adobe chapel where between thirty and forty people gathered every Sunday to read and study the Word, and that without fear.

The lecturer has in his possession the very copy of the Bible which was instrumental in the conversion of the first Mexican who ever became a Methodist preacher. The preacher over ten years ago went to his well-earned reward, but the book is still guarded as a treasure of unusual value.

Five years after the American war Santa Ana was recalled and appointed president "for one year." But this sufficed for him to get fast hold on the reins of government and to announce himself, as he did December 16, 1853, Permanent Dictator, with the modest title of "His Serene Highness." He recalled the Jesuits, who had been expelled during colonial times. The following July he sent José Gutierrez de Estrada to Europe, with powers "to negotiate in Europe for the establishment of a monarchy in Mexico." It would have been difficult in any country to have found a better tool of the Catholic Church. But Santa Ana was again deposed, and he fled the country in 1855. With him fell the unscrupulous Church party, and Estrada's scheme was checked for the time. General Álvarez, a true patriot, came to power, and selected for his secretary of justice, ecclesiastical affairs, and public instruction an Indian from the State of Oaxaca, Benito Juarez.

The first thing which General Álvarez and Mr. Juarez (the cultured and noble little Indian), aided by General Ignacio Comonfort, set about to accomplish was the framing of such a Constitution as would abolish the Concordat and establish religious freedom as the true foundation stone of a free and self-asserting nation. The result was that on the 5th of February, 1857, there was published, " in the name of God, and by the authority of the Mexican people," what Mr. Seward regarded as " the best instrument of its kind in the world," the Mexican Constitution, for the ample provisions of which many a faithful missionary in Mexico to-day lifts his heart to heaven in sincere gratitude.

The full text, well translated, may be seen in Dr.

Abbott's *Mexico and the United States*, but a synopsis of it is as follows:

1. The establishment of the constitutional federal government in the place of a military dictatorship.

2. Freedom and protection to slaves entering the national territory.

3. Freedom of religion.

4. Freedom of the press.

5. The nationalization of the $200,000,000 of property held by the clergy, from which, and other sources, the Church derived an annual income of not less than $20,000,000.

6. The subordination of the army to the civil power and the abolition of military and ecclesiastical *fueros*, or special tribunals.

7. The negotiation of commercial treaties of the fullest scope and most liberal character, including reciprocity of trade on our frontiers.

8. The colonization of Mexico by the full opening of every part of the country to immigration and the encouragement of foreign enterprise in every branch of industry, particularly in mining and in works of internal improvement.*

The immense wealth of the Church, aided by the ambassadors of France, Spain, and Guatemala, under the guidance of Clementi, nuncio of the pope,

* *Mexico in Transition*, p. 121.

effected the overthrow of Comonfort, and later on of Juarez. This resulted in the sending of Almonte, intimate friend of the archbishop, to the French court, where he was soon to plan, with Napoleon, the Papal-Franco intervention. In the meantime Miguel Miramon, an ardent instrument of the clergy, came to the presidency. Almonte negotiated with Napoleon III such a treaty as furnished the French emperor just the weapon he had long wanted, and "he gladly took its infamous author under his special protection, and resolved on a war whose injustice will be recognized as long as modern history is studied by honest men, and which can never be forgotten by Mexico." The Liberals captured some papers belonging to the Archbishop of Mexico in which Almonte was recommended to "the prayers and favors of the pope."

When Juarez and his government were reinstated in the national capital in January, 1861, many of the clergy left the country, accompanied by certain military traitors, and went directly to Paris to confer with Almonte and Napoleon.

The papal nuncio was bolder, and remained, only to be expelled from the country four days after Mr. Juarez had entered the national palace. Fortunate was it for Mexico that God raised up for her salvation such a man on the very eve of one of

INDEPENDENCE AND THE CONSTITUTION. 273

the greatest struggles ever known to a nation seeking freedom. This remarkable and well-beloved man was a pure Indian without a drop of Spanish blood in his veins. He was born in 1806, in a little Indian village twenty miles from the city of Oaxaca. When he first entered that city, a boy of twelve years, he was unable even to speak the Spanish language. He became an errand boy in the house of a lawyer, and this kind-hearted man, recognizing the worth of the boy, encouraged him to study. He did so, and soon became a student in the seminary of Oaxaca. From the seminary he graduated with honors, and was admitted to the bar in 1834. Eight years later he was elected chief justice of his native State, and soon after governor of the same. During his term of five years he made Oaxaca about the most prosperous State of Mexico. In 1846 he came to represent his State in the national Congress, when his wonderful qualifications for leadership were recognized by President Álvarez, who called him into the cabinet a few days later. So greatly did he distinguish himself in this position that he was soon made the standard bearer of the Liberal party and came to be, as Castelar said, "the saviour of the honor of his country." The Church early learned to fear him. When but a student the Conservative party, at that time having the upper hand in Oaxaca, consigned him to prison for his advocacy of liberal ideas and reform. In 1853 Santa Ana exiled him for the same reason; and we find him living for two years in New Orleans, where he endured great hardships on account of his poverty, earning a livelihood part of the time "by twisting cigars," while he improved the opportunity for closely studying our country and its institutions. The way opened for his return and restoration to office, and on the 12th of February, 1857, the Church fairly trembled before "the little Indian" as he hurled forth the famous "Reform Laws" with all the courage of a new Cromwell and all the ardor of a Luther. To these laws were added in September, 1873, and in January, 1877, certain additional provisions. The synopsis of all is as follows:

The absolute separation of Church and State.

Congress inhibited from the passage of any laws establishing or prohibiting any religion.

The free exercise of religious services. The State should not give official recognition to any religious festivals, save the Sabbath, as a day of rest.

Religious services were to be held only within the place of worship.

Clerical vestments were forbidden in the streets.

Religious processions were forbidden.

The use of church bells was restricted to calling the people to worship.

Pulpit discourses advising disobedience to the law, or injury to anyone, were strictly forbidden.

Worship in churches should be public only.

Gifts of real estate to religious institutions were declared unlawful, with the sole exception of edifices designed exclusively for the purposes of the institution.

The State would not recognize monastic orders nor permit their establishment.

The association of Sisters of Charity was suppressed in the republic; the Jesuits were expelled and not allowed to return.

Marriage was a civil contract and to be duly registered. The religious services might be added.

This Constitution and these Reform Laws provided for the confiscation of all Church property—including cathedrals, churches, chapels, convents, etc., and secured the expulsion of the Jesuits, Sisters of Charity, and all secret religious orders from the country. But the sun, moon, and stars continued to shine as brightly as ever.

LECTURE VIII.

NEW LIFE IN MEXICO.

LECTURE VIII.

NEW LIFE IN MEXICO.

BEFORE all had been accomplished, Almonte and Napoleon were preparing their pet plan to overthrow the republic and reestablish a monarchy and a State Church. It may not be amiss to look for a moment at this second character. Napoleon, when a youth, attempted to overthrow the French monarchy. Though pardoned by Louis Philippe he violated his compact and returned within two years to proclaim himself emperor. He was imprisoned for life, but escaped six years later, and made his way to England. On the establishment of the republic he returned to France, in 1848, and was elected a member of the Constitutional Assembly. On account of his loud profession of democratic sentiments he was elected president of the Assembly in December of that year, at which time he publicly swore, " In the presence of God and of the French people," to remain faithful to the democratic republic. But within three years he deliberately violated his oath, dissolved the National Assembly, placed the first military division in siege, scattered the Council of State, and became a despot over his country.

To this Victor Hugo adds these details: "At the same time Paris learned that fifteen of the inviolable representatives of the people had been arrested in their homes during the night by order of Louis Napoleon. In the days following he seized the executive power, made an attempt on the legislative power, drove away the Assembly, expelled the high court of justice, took twenty-five millions from the bank, gorged the army with gold, raked Paris with grapeshot, and terrorized France; he proscribed eighty-four of the representatives of the people, decreed despotism in fifty-eight articles under the title of a constitution; garroted the republic, made the sword of France a gag in the mouth of liberty, transported to Africa and Cayenne ten thousand democrats, exiled fifty thousand republicans, placed in all souls grief and on all foreheads blushes."* And this is the man with whom the pope had joined himself to work "wreck and ruin" on martyred Mexico. They were cautious enough to wait an opportune hour. They believed the hour had come when our country was engaged in one of the fiercest conflicts that ever rocked this world. It did not take them long to concoct a hollow pretext. They

* *The Destroyer of the Second Republic*, p. 29.

well knew that Mexico's treasury had been depleted by a succession of revolutions. Certain European citizens had loaned money to Mexico, and if they could get their respective governments to push the claims of the citizens they might in this, Mexico's weakest hour, possibly find a *casus belli*.

The plan worked well. The tripartite treaty was signed in London, October 31, 1861. The agents proceeded to Mexico, escorted by European gunboats, and had their interview with the secretary of state. It was ascertained that England's claim was $69,311,657, Spain's claim $9,461,986, while all the French claims, including the famous Jecker bonds, were $2,859,917. So the nation making the greatest ado was the one with the smallest claim. But when agents from England and Spain saw the situation, especially the Jesuitical workings of Napoleon's agent, and received Mexico's honest promise to pay, they washed their hands of the whole business and left Monsignor Saligny, the French Agent, alone to push his small claim—a ridiculous bagatelle for two nations to quarrel over.

Spain and England sent a handful of men as an escort of honor to their respective agents, but Napoleon, putting to shame the chivalry of France, sent seven thousand men to take care of their agent. But he had a secret object in view. Then the commission found the climate of Vera Cruz too hot and unhealthy, and united in a petition to President Juarez to be allowed to move themselves and their men to Orizaba, eighty-two miles from the coast and about four thousand feet above sea level. This was granted with the solemn promise to retire their troops on the conclusion of their work. When the British and Spanish envoys withdrew they begged the Frenchman to do the same. But he was acting under secret instructions. The emperor, Louis Napoleon, had now gained what he wanted, the power to act alone, on his own terms, in forcing his demands, at the bayonet's point, on an enemy whose generosity he had violated, while he demanded full payment of fictitious claims, and then drove him from the seat of authority to which the nation had elected him, in order to place upon it a stranger whom he had already selected for that purpose.

Mr. Juarez, taken by surprise, through the treachery of Napoleon's agent, whom he had treated in a friendly way, was forced to retire with his government to San Luis Potosí, later on to Chihuahua, and finally to El Paso, from which place, in case of necessity, he knew he could easily step over on American soil and seek protection for his life.

Before leaving Mexico, however, Congress conferred upon their trusted president "facultades extraordinarios," with the sole condition that on the return of peace he should inform the nation of the use he had made of such "unlimited authority."

In the meantime Maximilian, Archduke of Austria, accepted the mythical crown proffered by Napoleon. Notwithstanding the protests delivered by a special agent sent from Mr. Juarez, advising the archduke that the clerical party was deceiving him, and notwithstanding the experience of his brother Joseph with the pope only a few years before, he passed to Rome, receiving the blessing of Pius IX, and set sail for Mexico. The archbishop's agent in Europe assured him that his path would be "strewn with flowers from Vera Cruz to the throne in the halls of Moctezuma, that all opposition would drop into dust within a few weeks of his arrival," and that "the united nation would gather around him with enthusiasm as their beloved sovereign."

Subsequent events proved again to the world how completely Rome distorts the truth when it suits her plans. After all that happened it is not surprising that John Lothrop Motley, then American ambassador in Austria, wrote to his friend Oliver Wendell Holmes, saying:

"There is no glory in the grass nor verdure in anything. In fact, we have nothing green here but the Archduke Maximilian, who firmly believes that he is going forth to Mexico to establish an American empire, and that it is his divine mission to destroy the dragon of democracy and reestablish the true Church, the right divine, and all sorts of games. Poor young man!"*

The French troops, largely augmented, now rolled back the republican forces, the constitutional president had to retire, and Maximilian was installed by foreign bayonets. With the help of the archbishop, Labastida, the enthronement of Maximilian and Carlotta in the cathedral of the city of Mexico as emperor and empress was an eloquent display of pomp. The young emperor prepared to set up a gorgeous court on American soil. His estimate of annual expenses, including a modest salary of one and a half million for himself, five million for the clergy, and eight million for civil list and secret service, ran up to $36,681,000! With this financial scheme and the blessing of the pope he was to undertake the task of building up "a model Romish State on this continent" which was to be the entering wedge for general work of the same sort throughout the entire continent. In the light of these facts it is impossible to deny that Louis Napoleon and Pius IX contemplated a final subjuga-

* *Correspondence of J. L. Motley*, vol. ii, p. 138.

tion of this entire American hemisphere, north and south, to the papal see. This secret comes clearly out in a publication from the pen of Abbé Domenech, Maximilian's official press director, who in his book, *Mexico As It Is*, declares that the Monroe doctrine must be overthrown and the Latin race given a career on this continent. Then he adds, " If monarchy should be successfully introduced into Spanish republics in ten years the United States would themselves declare a dictatorship, which is a kind of republican monarchy adopted by degenerate or too revolutionary republics." *

We beg to refer you again to *Mexico in Transition* for perhaps the most full and correct account of the so-called French intervention found in the English language. Especially complete is it as to its relation to the pope on one hand, and to the possibilities of establishing evangelical missions in Mexico on the other. But we hasten with our story.

The Confederacy, under Jefferson Davis, sought recognition from Maximilian, and in order to obtain it his forces along the Texas border acted as allies to the emperor by intercepting bearers of dispatches between President Juarez and his minister at Washington. When at last Lee surrendered and the Confederacy collapsed intercourse was opened and

* Quoted from *Mexico in Transition*, p. 173.

made secure between Washington and the Mexican frontier. One of the first things done by our noble Lincoln was to send a letter full of sympathy and inspiration to Benito Juarez, who was viewing his land in the hand of invaders, the institutions so dearly loved "trampled under the feet of men," while he anxiously awaited a turn of events in the little town of El Paso del Norte. In this note Lincoln in substance said, "Be of good cheer, dear friend, Mexico will rise again."

On December 16, 1865, Mr. Seward sent through our ambassador at Paris a rather brief but effective note to the French court. In polite but pointed language Mr. Seward makes two statements, and then concludes: "Having thus frankly stated our position, I leave the question for the consideration of France, sincerely hoping that that great nation may find it compatible with its best interests and high honor to withdraw from its aggressive attitude in Mexico within some convenient and reasonable time, and thus leave the people of that country to the free enjoyment of the system of republican government they have established for themselves, and of their adhesion to which they have given what seems to the United States to be decisive and conclusive as well as touching proof."[*]

[*] *Diplomatic Correspondence of the United States*, 1865, p. 451.

NEW LIFE IN MEXICO. 287

No more effective "shot" was ever fired from Washington than that note. The Monroe doctrine was not a dead letter. Napoleon realized it, and his troops were withdrawn. The Empress Carlotta flew to Europe. Disappointed and enraged to the verge of madness by her cool reception from Napoleon, she hastened to Rome in the vain hope that the pope could supply men and means to sustain her husband and the empire in Mexico. What happened during that mysterious interview "of one hour and eighteen minutes" perhaps the world may never know, but poor Carlotta left the Vatican a raving maniac, and, though somewhat calmer, she has never yet regained her reason. Nor does she know to this day the sad fate of Maximilian, as she rambles in her lonely garden at the Castle of Miramar.

When at last Maximilian realized the loss of the French troops, and that Napoleon and Pius IX feared to furnish further aid, he reached the conclusion that the empire was a failure. He desired himself then to leave the country.

He quietly moved to Orizaba, under pretext of a change of climate, but with the purpose of improving the first opportunity of returning to Europe. The question of abdication, insisted upon by Marshal Bazaine, delayed him long enough to allow the Clericals to arrange another desperate blow at republican institutions. Two well-known generals, Marquez and Miramon, champions of the Church party, were to raise a native army (against which the United States could not protest) to prop up the empire. In a mysterious way money became suddenly plentiful. The Church furnished it. Maximilian returned to the city of Mexico rather against his will, now only a passive tool and little better than a prisoner in the hands of the Clerical party.

The United States government had firmly insisted that no French troops should remain beyond March 11, 1867, and General Sheridan had reached the Rio Grande with American troops to aid Mr. Juarez in case of necessity. Maximilian realized his great mistake in returning. The funds were soon exhausted; the native army ready to support the empire was not forthcoming, so the emperor, the archbishop, and the traitor generals found themselves with but two cities in their hands, Mexico and Querétaro. From the first Maximilian was soon driven and took refuge in the second, possibly with the hope of ultimately reaching American soil, where his life, at least, might be spared.

Querétaro was soon captured by General Escobedo, and Maximilian, the tool of Napoleon, the puppet of Pius IX, was a prisoner. He was fairly tried and condemned to be shot. Some have thought the penalty extreme, but it must be remembered that he was a foreign invader and the usurper of the rights of a sovereign people; that by force of arms he had disposed of the rights and lives of thousands of Mexicans; that he had, by decree (October 3, 1865), falsely declared the republican army a band of robbers whose president and government had abandoned the national territory, and that he continued " to employ means of violence, death, and destruction until he fell."

Besides all this there was no heir, and here was the empire in a nutshell. "Allow him to go now," Mr. Juarez said, "and there was no knowing what the pope and some European power might contrive in future. No; the lesson has been a dear one for us, and we must now teach a corresponding one to Pius IX, Napoleon, and all the world."

Sebastian Lerdo de Tejada, secretary of state under Juarez, closed his reply to the lawyers of Maximilian, when the appeal for pardon was reiterated, in the following words:

" The existence of Mexico as an independent nation must not be left to the will of the governments of Europe. Our reforms, our progress, our liberty must not stop at the wish of any foreign sovereign who might take a notion to impose an emperor upon us who would attempt again to regulate the amount of liberty or servitude he thought best to bestow upon us. The life of Maximilian might be the excuse for an attempt at a viceroyalty. The return of Maximilian to Europe might be a weapon for the calumniators and enemies of Mexico to bring about a restoration and the overthrow of the institutions of the country. For nearly fifty years Mexico has pursued a policy of pardon and leniency, and the fruits of that policy have been anarchy among ourselves and loss of prestige abroad. Now, or never, may the republic consolidate itself."

Every appeal to spare his life, including that of the Emperor of Austria, that of the Queen of England, and the impassionate and repeated pleas by the Princess Salm-Salm, as well as the carefully drawn request of our Mr. Seward, were all in vain. Every attempt to bribe the officers, one of them accompanied by no less a price than $200,000, failed. An aggrieved and wronged nation, weeping by thousands for those who had suffered and died through him, demanded justice. So after a fair trial, in which the best judicial talent in the country, and of his own selection, vainly defended him, the Archduke Maximilian, of Austria, was executed on

NEW LIFE IN MEXICO. 291

the little " Hill of the Bells " just outside the city of Querétaro.

When Mr. Juarez, the legal President of Mexico and leader of the Liberal party, returned from his exile and was again in possession of the office to which he had been elevated by his people, he turned his attention to the party which brought so much sorrow and destruction to the nation. The great Church property had already been nationalized. Its value was estimated, as already stated, at from $200,000,000 to $300,000,000. From this and other sources the Church had derived an annual income of $20,000,000. The Liberals took the ground that this immense property had been unjustly wrung out of the hands of the people, and therefore should be returned to its lawful owners. As many churches were designated for public worship as were needed for that purpose. But these were only leased to the Church party for a term of ninety-nine years. The title is still vested in the government, and on more than one occasion it has been necessary to remind the clergy who is the owner of these properties. The occasion of this kind causing most astonishment occurred when Señor José Baz, governor of the Federal District, learning that the bishop was preaching against the Liberals and the reform laws, rode on horseback at the head of a body of men into the Cathedral, arrested the bishop, turned the people into the street, locked the door, and carried the key to his own office. This episode brought about a clear understanding between the interested parties before the key was given up. Henceforth treason must not be preached in Mexican churches.

Much of the property—convents, monasteries, houses of religious orders, and the Inquisition—was sold to help the national treasury. Many edifices were given to army officers in payment of long years of service. It can be easily imagined that this policy created a large army of opponents to the Church as a political institution.

The Liberal party was given hearty cooperation from the masses of the people, and rightly so. The lessons of the Inquisition, the demands upon their hard-earned and limited living through the confessional and the seven so-called sacraments, had laid burdens upon them " grievous to be borne." True, the Inquisition was broken up, but the remains of it were seen in places of religious retreat, while many of the milder instruments of torture were used not only in these retreats, but imposed upon the people in the churches and in their own homes.

Madame Calderon de la Barca, wife of the first

Spanish ambassador to Mexico—Spain having consented to recognize the independence of her lost province—during her stay in the country wrote a series of letters which were afterward edited and published by Prescott, the historian. She was a Roman Catholic, and describes the use of these instruments as she saw it in the Church of Santo Domingo. She says:

"The scene was curious. About one hundred and fifty men, enveloped in cloaks and serapes, their faces entirely concealed, were assembled in the body of the church. A monk had just mounted the pulpit, and the church was dimly lighted, except where he stood in bold relief, with his gray robes and cowl thrown back, giving a full view of his high, bald forehead and expressive face. His discourse was a rude but very forcible and eloquent description of the torments prepared in hell for impenitent sinners. The effect of the whole was very solemn. It appeared like the preparation for the execution of a multitude of condemned criminals. When the discourse was finished they all joined in prayer with much fervor and enthusiasm, beating their breasts and falling upon their faces. Then the monk stood up and in a very distinct voice read several passages of Scripture descriptive of the sufferings of Christ. The organ then struck up the

'Miserere,' and all of a sudden the church was plunged in profound darkness—all but a sculptured representation of the crucifixion, which seemed to hang in the air illuminated. I felt rather frightened, and would have been very glad to leave the church, but it would have been impossible in the darkness. Suddenly a terrible voice in the dark cried, 'My brothers, when Christ was fastened to the pillar by the Jews he was scourged.' At these words the bright figure disappeared and the darkness became total. Suddenly we heard the sound of hundreds of scourges descending upon the bare flesh. I cannot conceive anything more horrible. Before ten minutes had passed the sound became splashing, from the blood that was flowing. We could not leave the church, but it was perfectly sickening; and had I not been able to take hold of the señora's hand and feel something human beside me I could have fancied myself transported into a congregation of evil spirits. Now and then, but very seldom, a suppressed groan was heard, and occasionally the voice of the monk encouraging them by ejaculations or by short passages from Scripture. Sometimes the organ struck up, and the poor wretches, in a faint voice, tried to join in the 'Miserere.' The sound of the scourging is indescribable. At the end of half an hour a little bell was rung, and the voice of the monk was heard calling upon them to desist; but such was their enthusiasm that the horrible lashing continued louder and fiercer than ever. In vain he entreated them not to kill themselves, and assured them that Heaven would be satisfied, and that human nature could not endure beyond a certain point. No answer, but the loud sound of the scourges, which are many of them of iron, with sharp points that enter the flesh. At length, as if they were perfectly exhausted, the sound grew fainter, and little by little ceased altogether. We then got up, and, with great difficulty, groped our way in the pitch darkness till we reached the door. They say that the church floor was frequently covered with blood after one of these penances, and that a man died the other day in consequence of his wounds."

These *disciplinas, silicias,* circlets, or crowns, and waistbands are in a quiet way still imposed upon the blind dupes of the priests.* The administration of the seven sacraments was a source of great revenue to the Church, and a means by which thousands were kept in poverty. None of these, unless it was in the case of "holy orders"

* Specimens of these different articles of self-punishment were exhibited by the lecturer, who had obtained some of them from converts who aforetime used them.

(and of these we are in doubt), were ever administered without the payment of an extravagant fee to the priest. The poorest of the poor were obliged to pay for baptism, confirmation, the eucharist, penance, matrimony, or extreme unction a sum equivalent to from ten to fifteen dollars of our money. The multitudes of peons working on the great estates were the principal sufferers from this oppressive simony. These estates were visited periodically by the priests, and the sacraments were administered by wholesale. At the end of his day's work the priest would present his bill to the administrator and receive his pay in bulk. The administrator, in turn, charged up to the individual laborer his part or parts—for the same family may have asked for two or three sacraments. Now, this poor man probably earned a sum equivalent to thirty cents of our money, and, counting out the Sabbath and other feast days, of which there were many, worked about two hundred days or less in the year. At best this would give him sixty dollars per year. From this he must clothe and feed his family, buying his provisions at a store owned by his employer (where prices were certainly not lower than elsewhere), meet a small tax, perhaps, for doctor and medicines, and pay besides the exorbitant exactions of the mercenary priesthood. The exception was to find a man out of debt, and consequently out of slavery, for there existed a law prohibiting the laborer to leave his employer while indebted to him; so unless a new master came forward he was likely to be in debt until freed by death itself. Thus it often happened that grim death, with all his terrors for the superstitious mind, was a better friend to man than was his fellow.

Among the higher class of people the confessional and "last sacrament" were the chief sources of bonanza. Sins might be atoned for and the poor sinner's peace made with the Church by the payment of silver and gold. And when the "faithful," taught from infancy that without extreme unction he could not possibly enter heaven, came down to death's door the father confessor was at his side. In one hand the "sacrament" was held and often with the other this so-called man of God would shake over the trembling soul the pains of purgatory and the terrors of hell till a good portion of his worldly goods was made over to the Church—custodian of heaven's key! These expressions are fully justified by the testimony of a Roman Catholic author, Abbé Domenech, the chief chaplain of the French army, who, in his *Mexico As It Is*, declares concerning the priests, that "they make merchandise of the sacrament, and make money by every religious ceremony." Then he adds: "One of the greatest evils in Mexico is the exorbitant fee for the marriage ceremony. The priests compel the poor to live without marriage by demanding for the nuptial benediction more than a Mexican mechanic, with his slender wages, can accumulate in fifty years of strictest economy. This is no exaggeration."

Thus writes a faithful son of the Church. But the Liberal party, under Comonfort and Juarez, sought to remedy these excesses and set their people free as far as within their power. Hence, on being reinstated in the national capital, the laws of reform (already quoted in substance) were enlarged and reenacted in order to carry out the provisions and purposes of the Constitution. Under the protection of both Protestant missionaries were enabled to enter Mexico. Mr. Juarez, on more than one occasion, manifested, publicly and privately, his obligations to God and the desire that the representatives of a pure form of Christianity should obtain among the millions of his priest-ridden countrymen. At the close of the French intervention he issued the following proclamation:

"Let the Mexican people fall on their knees before God, who has deigned to crown our arms with victory. He has smitten the foreigner who has oppressed us sorely. He has established these, his people, in their rightful place. For he who hath his habitation in the heavens is the visitor and protector of our country, who strikes down those who came to do us ill. The excellent, the only just, almighty, and eternal One is he who hath dispersed the nations which, like vultures, had fallen on Mexico."

One of our native preachers, an ex-priest, enjoyed the personal friendship of Mr. Juarez up to the time of his death, and to him the lamented president once said: " Upon the development of Protestantism largely depends the future of our country."

No wonder we find the authorities, including the president and the State governors, as a rule, ready to give due protection to the lives and properties of the missionaries. The first missionary to enter the field was a brave Christian woman. In the early fifties Miss Melinda Rankin went to reside in Brownsville, Texas. While studying the Spanish language she employed some Mexicans to act as colporteurs among their country people. Later she moved as far south as Monterey, where she established a day and boarding school. In this she seems to have had a biblical department (the first theological seminary under evangelical auspices in the republic of Mexico), for the youth were taught not only the rudiments of a common education, but received daily instruction in the truths of the Gospel. After a while some of the older boys were sent every Sabbath into the towns and villages about Monterey to read and explain the chapter of God's word which they had been studying during the week. In time it was found that fourteen little congregations had grown up through her instrumentality, and our theological professoress had thus providentially come to be the pastor and bishop of hundreds of souls, while her infant flock looked up to her with just as much regard and reverence, perhaps, as if some bishop or council had laid "holy hands" on her head. When her health failed her work was handed over to the Presbyterians. Later some of the workers came as far south as Villa de Cos, in the State of Zacatecas, where they were greatly encouraged by Dr. Prevost, a Christian physician living in the capital of that State. He was an American, and in his long residence in Mexico he has been a most valued adviser and helper in the Presbyterian Mission.

Several of the evangelical Churches in the United States decided to enter the field toward the close of 1872. They did so in about the following order: the Presbyterian, Methodist Episcopal, Congregational, Baptist (Southern Convention), Southern Methodist, Southern Presbyterian, Reformed As-

NEW LIFE IN MEXICO. 301

sociate Presbyterian, Baptist (Northern Convention), the Friends, and the Cumberland Presbyterian. Besides these there were several independent missions, such as the Church of Jesus, part of which, about ten years ago, was formally taken up by the Episcopalians; an English mission originated by the late James Pascoe, but since his death dismembered; and finally the work of a Mr. Harris, in Orizaba. Of these smaller independent missions it has been impossible to secure reliable statistics; but after months of persistent correspondence we are able to present the following surprising results in our sister republic of a little over twenty years:

TWENTY YEARS OF SYSTEMATIC EVANGELICAL WORK.*

	Total of all Missions.	Methodist Episcopal Missions.
I. The Field.		
Number of centers of operation............	87	30
Number of congregations..................	609	133
II. The Workers.		
Number of ordained foreign missionaries....	59	10
Number of assistant foreign missionaries (that is, unordained men, and wives of ordained and assistant missionaries)....	59	10
Number of foreign lady teachers...........	67	8
Whole number of foreign workers..........	185	28
Number of native preachers, ordained......	111	15
Number of native preachers, unordained....	164	33
Number of native teachers.......	177	38
Number of other native helpers............	94	56
Total number of native workers...........	546	142
Grand total of foreign and native workers...	731	160

* During these years the British and American Bible societies have distributed 416,819 volumes of sacred writ in Mexico.

	Total of all Missions.	Methodist Episcopal Missions.
III. The Churches.		
Number of churches organized............	441	133
Number of communicants................	16,034	3,085
Number of probable adherents............	49,512	8,214
IV. The Schools.		
Number of training and theological schools.	9	1
Number of students in same.............	86	7
Number of boarding schools or orphanages.	33	3
Number of pupils in same...............	625	56
Number of common schools..............	116	48
Number of pupils in same...............	6,709	3,190
Total number under instruction..........	7,336	3,253
Number of Sunday schools...............	347	59
Number of Sunday school teachers and officers................................	694	157
Number of Sunday school scholars........	9,813	1,797
Total membership of Sunday schools......	10,507	1,944
V. Publishing Interests.		
Number of publishing houses............	10	1
Number of papers issued................	13	1
Pages of all kinds of religious literature issued since the establishment of your press................................	159,948,246	40,048,246
VI. Properties.		
Number of church buildings.............	118	28
Approximate value of same (including furniture)................................	635,550	104,700
Number of parsonages..................	$30	18
Approximate value of same (including society furniture)...........................	217,900	128,200
Number of educational buildings.........	31	8
Approximate value of same (including furniture and utensils)....................	283,885	117,200
Value of publishing outfit...............	40,150	12,850
Total value of all missionary property.....	1,101,485	362,950
VII. Historic and Personal.		
How many martyrs, if any, has your mission had?................................	58	4
Place and date of such martyrdom?.......		

NEW LIFE IN MEXICO. 303

These 609 congregations, 16,000 communicants, and nearly 50,000 adherents, with 6,709 children in our day schools and 9,813 in our Sunday schools, are the work of only about twenty years. And all this has been accomplished in a land where a few years ago there was no open Bible, no Protestant school, and no evangelical Church. " This is the Lord's doings, and it is marvelous in our eyes."

In the early forties Madame Calderon de la Barca, a devout Roman Catholic as already said, writing of the disturbed and unsatisfactory condition of the country and the people, and writing, too, when there was not a declared Protestant in all the land, said, " Let them (the clergy) beware lest half a century later they be awakened from their delusion and find the Cathedral turned into a meeting house and all painted white, the railing melted down, the Virgin's jewels sold to the highest bidder, the floor washed (which would do it no harm), and around the whole a new wooden paling, freshly done in green, and all this performed by some of the artists from the wide-awake republic further north." If the màdame could rise from her grave and return to Mexico she would be surprised to know what a real prophetess she was. The "railing" of solid silver was melted during the War of Independence, the government recently put a substantial paling, the floor has been washed often, the unaccompanied mass of other days is now often followed by a sermon, sometimes even a gospel sermon; for Rome is always forced to preach when Protestantism is planted in her midst. And besides all this evangelical Churches are multiplying more and more in every State of the republic, and the Gospel now having "free course" in this land of Moctezuma, its influence will soon spread into the central and the northern part of South America till we meet our brother missionaries of those regions, and all Spanish America will be lifted up into the life and liberty of the children of God.

Our own branch of the Christian Church was one of the first to enter the field, and it seems to have been providentially guided in the selection of important centers and the building up of suitable headquarters. Our experience in the city of Mexico will suffice as an illustration of this fact. Here, as our first superintendent graphically tells us in his recent work on Mexico, we own a portion of the Convent of San Francisco, and it stands on the very spot where Moctezuma's pleasure palace stood four hundred years ago. After the nationalization of all the country's great Church property this part of the immense convent, covering what is equivalent to four city blocks, became a circus, then a theater, later it served as the national Congress hall, and then again as a theater. This theater company failed just as our first superintendent reached the city of Mexico in February, 1873. In a strange and certainly providential way, as described in the tenth chapter of his book, this property, with its recent improvements, became one of the most complete Protestant headquarters in the republic. It is centrally located, contains church, chapel, boys' schoolrooms, press, bookstore, editorial and agent's rooms, and three parsonages. All these in place of pagan palace and Romish convent. Mexico has had many transitions during the past twenty-five years, but none more wonderful than that which we witness here.

And this is especially so when, in the very corridors which formerly served for the solemn processions and awful deeds of Spanish friars, you can now find several times a week a devout and happy Methodist congregation under their own roof, with "none to molest," as they worship God just as you do here in this highly favored land. No wonder that Bishop FitzGerald, sitting in the chapel pulpit and looking out on the ardent worshipers with perhaps some of their same thoughts running through his mind, was carried on the wings of song more than once into a shouting mood.

Now let us examine the following contrast: Thirty years ago Pope Pius IX and the Jesuits, Napoleon and Eugénie, Maximilian and Carlotta, were banded together for the establishment of a European monarchy in Mexico, which meant the complete extermination of the Liberal party, the reenthronement of the Clericals, and the unlimited sorrow and destruction of the people and the nation.

On the collapse of the empire in Mexico, Europe was still in commotion. The troops of Louis Napoleon were in Rome, but were soon after withdrawn under a secretly arranged treaty between Napoleon and Victor Emmanuel. On the 18th of July, 1870, the pope's claim to infallibility was decreed. The very next day, as Mr. Gladstone says, " Napoleon III, the political ally and supporter of Pius IX, unchained the furies of war, which in a few weeks swept away the empire of France, and with it the temporal power of the infallible pope, while the five hundred and thirty-three purblind Catholic bishops who had voted for infallibility made a hasty and ignominious retreat from Rome.

On the 1st of September following France was completely crushed at Sedan by her ancient Germanic foe. On the 31st of the same month Victor Emmanuel, who had recently been excommunicated by the pope, entered Rome at the head of the Liberal army, and in a few days was almost unanimously chosen as the ruler of a free and united people. Every ruler in Europe turned a deaf ear to the impassionate appeals of the pope for reinstatement in power. He was now only a poor prisoner, his capital taken from him, and his outrageous assumptions had fallen to the dust, and to-day a dozen Protestant churches are found within the walls of that capital, one of which was located, by Dean Vernon, conveniently near the Vatican.

Napoleon III had long sought a quarrel with Germany, and at last it came. On the 1st of September, 1870, this " eldest son of the Church," after seeing his forces completely vanquished, was taken prisoner at Sedan by a Protestant king and carried in exile to the Castle of Wilhelmshohe, " never to wear a crown again." Paris was soon captured, Alsace and Lorraine ceded to Germany, and the Rhine made the permanent boundary between the two countries. All this news was sent to Wilhelmshohe for the comfort of the proud spirit who hoped, like his uncle, to be the dictator of Europe, and who only eight years before had pompously declared that he would open a career for the " Latin race, and all that it implies, on the soil of the New World," which was to be " the most glorious enterprise of the nineteenth century." "The power behind the throne" was the Empress Eugénie, "a frivolous Spanish bigot," an eager partisan of the pope. She it was who received every year, on Palm Sunday, from the holy father, "a palm branch, blessed by him, which was hung at the head of her bed as a protection from evil during the year." She was a ready tool in the hands of the Jesuits, and had influenced Napoleon in his inimical relation to Italy and Mexico. She believed her husband was the providential instrument to crush Protestant Germany and aid the pope in all his plans, and exultantly exclaimed as Napoleon started for Sedan, "This is my war."

But in a few days she was glad to accept the aid of a foreigner in her secret escape from Paris, and to be allowed to make her home in England. She was enraged over the thought of free Italians in Rome, humiliated as the Prussians entered Paris, and depressed beyond measure as she saw herself perfectly helpless to prevent, a short time later, the establishment of Protestant missions in the very capital where, in such royal magnificence, she had spent the proudest days of her romantic life. When Napoleon died, in 1873, she clung to her only son, "the Prince Imperial," concerning whom she had great hopes for the future. But soon we see

NEW LIFE IN MEXICO. 309

Eugénie alone in Africa, with her dead son, "discrowned, widowed, and childless, a sad but striking memorial of the penalty dealt out to the oppressors of Mexico."

Maximilian's sad fate has already been explained. Carlotta still lives in Miramar, hopelessly insane. And the Jesuits, behind the united efforts of Napoleon and the pope, have been driven from nearly every land in Christendom, and even from some heathen lands. The United States of America some day may have to follow the example of these in defense of her blood-bought legacies of freedom.

Now look, for a moment, at the country these had all united to crush. Shortly after the fall of Maximilian, Mexico became a united, happy, and prosperous nation. For seventeen years she has enjoyed uninterrupted peace, and most of the time under the presidency of a man who would readily make a leader among the statesmen of any nation of earth—General Porfirio Diaz—friend of every modern idea that will lift up his country, and repeatedly pledged, by his own spontaneous volition, to extend to all Protestant workers the full protection of the law. When the so-called empire fell less than one hundred miles of railroad existed in the country, while now we have six thousand eight hundred and seventy-seven miles. At that time only the chief towns (not including all the State capitals) were connected by telegraph wire, while now there are twenty-five thousand four hundred and seventy-six miles of such wire, putting every town of any importance in direct communication with the national capital, and consequently with the outside world.

Then there was but one bank, and that not a bank of issue, whereas now we have a dozen, whose capital and business will compare favorably with those of our own country. Interest on the foreign debt is being promptly met, and Mexico's credit abroad is most excellent, as was recently proven by the eagerness with which her loan of £3,000,000 was taken up in Berlin.

The scheme for draining the valley, so long delayed, is now being pushed to conclusion, at a total cost of $15,000,000 (silver), and will make the city of Mexico one of the healthiest on the continent. For the fiscal year ending June 30, 1893, Mexico produced $48,500,000 worth of silver, or double the annual output of fifteen years ago. Mining costs only a fraction of what it costs in the United States. The gold output last year was $1,400,000. Iron is plentiful. Coal, copper, lead, and nearly all the precious and baser metals are found. Factories are going up in many places—plants at Monterey and San Luis Potosí costing nearly a million dollars each (silver), at San Rafael a full million, while the new cotton and print works at Orizaba are worth three and a half millions.

The worthy president is especially interested in educational matters, as witness the University and Normal School of Mexico city, as well as the new and well-equipped normal schools, open to both sexes, in Jalapa, Oaxaca, Durango, Guadalajara, and other places.

Foreign capital is flowing freely into the country to buy some of their excellent tropical lands, for the purpose of raising coffee, vanilla, sugar, and fruits. Five millions (gold) went last year into one district alone for the purchase of coffee. No wonder that exports have doubled in the past fifteen years.

Able men have represented Mexico in the recent International Medical Congress at Washington, Chicago, and Rome, while at the great Silver Congress of Europe every utterance of her delegates commanded closest attention. The Columbian Exposition awarded one thousand one hundred and seventy-seven prizes to Mexican exhibits. We might continue on this line, but surely this is enough to make clear our point.

'About a year after Columbus came to these shores Pope Alexander VI assumed to divide the western world between the Spanish and the Portuguese. Soon after Isabel, "the poetic and Catholic queen," made her last will and testament. In this interesting instrument we find the following paragraph: "When we were granted by the most holy apostolic see the islands and continents of the great ocean, discovered and to be discovered, our principal intention was, as we prayed from Pope Alexander VI, of blessed memory, who made us the grant, to endeavor to induce and bring the peoples thereof by conversion to the holy Catholic faith, and to send to said islands and continents prelates and ecclesiastics, clergymen and gifted persons fearing God, to instruct the residents thereof in the Catholic faith, showing them and instructing them in good doctrine and customs, and pay such attention thereto as is explained more at length in the letters of grant. Very affectionately I pray the king, my lord, and beg of the princess, my daughter, and her husband, the prince, that they may so do and ordain, and that this may be their principal aim; that they may place especial attention therein, and that they do not permit nor allow the neighboring Indians and inhabitants of the islands and continents, conquered and to be conquered, to receive injury in their persons, but that they be justly and well treated; and should they have received any hurt or injury, that the same be repaired and atoned for, so that nothing may be done beyond that ordained in our Apostolic Letters of Credence."

To this solemn legacy the Roman Catholic Church has been wofully recreant, losing one of the sublimest opportunities ever placed within the reach of any Church. In the providence of God this country now looks to us. In Mexico are twelve million souls; beyond, in Central and South America, are about fifty millions more, making, in all, over sixty millions.

Not one European missionary is found working in their midst. Nor will such ever probably work south of the Rio Grande. Methodism, in common with all evangelical Churches of the United States, has the high privilege and solemn duty of helping to lift up and evangelize these millions; every door is open, and further progress toward this glorious consummation depends only upon the liberality of our people. Bishop Newman never uttered a more important truth than when in New York he recently said, "I believe that God has placed in our responsibility all this continent."

Mexico long ago took its place in the galaxy of

civilized nations. Let its State and local authorities cooperate heartily with the central government in the protection of modern industries, of educational advantages, and religious liberty; let its schools multiply, let its free press extend everywhere, let evangelical church spires multiply throughout its beautiful vales and on its noble mountain sides, and then the land of Moctezuma, of Hidalgo, of Juarez, and of Diaz will arise in all the strength of its new life to recognize as its chief ruler and divine guide " the King of kings and Lord of lords."

INDEX.

Abbott, Gorham D., 31.
Acosta, José de, 24.
Almonte, 272, 279.
Amaquemacan, 144, 146.
"Anonymous Conqueror, The," 23.
"Atlantic," etymology of word, 60.
Atlantis, 56.
Audience, 235.
Augustine I, 259.
Authorities, list of, 23-31.
Aztecs, their route to Mexico, 156-161.
Aztlan, 151.
Bancroft, Hubert H., 30.
Boturini, Lorenzo Benaduci, 26.
Bravo, episode of, 254, 255.
Brinton, criticised, 18.
" Burning the ships," 224.
Calderon, Madame, 31, 292, 293, 303.
Calendar, Mexican, 133, 134.
Calendar stone, 77.
California, sale of, 266.
Carlota, 287.
Carthaginian theory of population, 55.
Cempoala, Cortez at, 215.
Chichimecs, 126, 144-150.
Chinese, origin of population, 71.
Cholula, pyramid of, 110, 113, 229.
Clavigero, Francisco Javier, 27.
Coat of arms, 159.
Color, variety of, 39.
Comonfort, 270, 272, 298.
Constitution of 1814, 253.
Constitution of 1857, 270, 271.
Cortez, biographical sketch, 201-205; arrival in Mexico, 206; receives embassy, 210-215; overthrows idols, 215-220; conspiracy against, 221-224;
burns his ships, 224, 225; at Tlaxcala, 226-228; victor, 230.
Cozumel, Cortez at, 218.
Creation, Quiche account of, 95, 96.
Cross, symbol of, 25, 116, 117.
Cuautemoc, monument to, 4-7.
Diaz, Bernal, 23.
Diaz, Porfirio, 309-315.
Egyptian theory of Mexicans, 51.
" Fair God," 117, 119, 138-143.
Ferdinand VII, 245, 257, 258.
French interference, 279-291.
Gage, Thomas, 27.
Greek theory of population, 49.
" Grito de Dolores," 248.
Herrera, A. de, 24.
Hidalgo, 246-252.
Hindoo origin of population, 71.
Huehue Tlapallan, 123.
Hueman, 128-131, 140.
Huitzilopochtli, 157, 160, 167, 190, 229.
Humboldt, Alexander Von, 28.
Independence, struggle for, 246-259.
Irish theory of population, 47.
Isabella's will, 312.
Iturbide, 258, 259.
Ixtlilxochitl, 24.
Japanese origin of population, 73.
Jewish theory of population, 67.
Juarez, 270, 272-274, 282-291, 298, 299.
Kingsborough, Lord, 29.
Language, diversity of, 39.
Las Casas, B. de, 24.
Leif, son of Eric, 51.
Madoc-ap-Owen, 44.
Marina, 209.
Maximilian, 283, 284, 290.
Maya, 86-92, 105.

INDEX.

Maya-Quiche, 86–88, 92.
Mayer, Brantz, 31.
Metals, production of precious, 191.
Mexican War, 266, 269.
Mexico city founded, 160, 165; derivation of name, 167.
Mexitli, 161, 167.
Mining, 310.
Miramon, 272, 288.
Missions, 299–314.
Moctezuma I, 174, 177.
Moctezuma II, 178–187; sends gifts to Cortez, 210–215.
Morelos, 253.
Mormon account of Mexicans, 66.
Motolinia, 23.
Naphtuhim, 52, 54.
Napoleon I, 244.
Napoleon III, 272, 279–284, 307–309.
Nationalization of Church property, 291, 292.
Nezahualcoyotl, 170–173.
Norse theory of population, 50.
Numidian theory of population, 56.
Olmecs, 113–119.
Ophir, location of, 75.
Origin of Mexicans, 35–80; autochthonic theory, 35–43; European theories, 44–51; African theories, 52; Asiatic theories, 64–80; diverse origin, 83.
Otomís, 119.
Paintings, importance of, 10; collections of, 13.
Palenque, 106, 114.
Papantzin, Doña Maria, 188.
Phœnician origin of population, 74.
Plan of Iguala, 258.
Popol Vuh, 94, 95.
Prehistoric Mexicans, 83–120.
Prescott, William H., 29.
Pulque, 137.
Quetzalcoatl, 117–119, 191.

Quetzalcohuatl, 125.
Quiche, 92–95.
Quinames, 108.
Railroads, 309.
Ramirez, on Mexico's debt to Spain, 231.
Rankin, Miss Melinda, 299.
Records, destruction of, 9; completeness of, 10; collections of, 13.
Reform laws, the, 274, 275.
Robertson, William, 27.
Roman theory of population, 50.
Sahagun, Bernardino de, 24.
Santa Ana, 260–262, 269.
Scandinavian theory of population, 50.
Scotch theory of population, 48.
Scourging, 293.
Seward's note to France, 286.
Short, John T., 31.
Siguenza y Gongora, Carlos de, 25.
Statistics, 301.
St. Thomas in Mexico, 118, 119.
Telegraphs, 310.
"Ten Lost Tribes," 67.
Tenoch, 166, 168.
Tenochtitlan, 160.
Teoamoxtli, 131, 132.
Teoicpalli, 157.
Tezcatlipoca, 140–143.
Tezcoco, 145, 168, 169.
Thompson, Waddy, 31.
Tlaxcala taken, 226.
Tlaxcalans, 153–155.
Toltecs, 123–127.
Torquemada, Juan de, 25.
Totonacs, 119.
Tula, ruins of, 19–21, 101, 104, 129, 130, 135, 136.
Victor Emmanuel, 306.
Victoria, 260.
Votan, 89.
Welsh theory of Mexicans, 44.
Wilson, R. A., 32.
Xicalancas, 113–119.
Yucatan, Mayas of, 105.

www.ingramcontent.com/pod-product-compliance
Lightning Source LLC
Chambersburg PA
CBHW030012240426
43672CB00007B/926